MW01025691

TO:

_____

FROM:

_____

DATE:

_____

POCKETFUL OF
Bible
Promises
FOR
Godly Women

LIVE YOUR FAITH

Bible Translations Used:

HCSB: Scripture quotations marked HCSB® are taken from the Holman Christian Standard Bible®, Copyright © 1999, 2000, 2002, 2003, 2009 by Holman Bible Publishers. Used by permission. HCSB® is a federally registered trademark of Holman Bible Publishers.

ICB: Scripture taken from The Holy Bible, International Children's Bible® Copyright© 1986, 1988, 1999, 2015 by Tommy Nelson™, a division of Thomas Nelson. Used by permission.

KJV: Scripture quotations taken from The Holy Bible, King James Version.

NASB: Scripture quotations taken from the New American Standard Bible®, Copyright © 1960, 1962, 1963, 1968, 1971, 1972, 1973, 1975, 1977, 1995 by The Lockman Foundation Used by permission.

NCV: Scripture taken from the New Century Version. Copyright © 1987, 1988, 1991 by Thomas Nelson, Inc. Used by permission. All rights reserved.

NIV: Scripture quotations marked (NIV) are taken from the Holy Bible, New International Version®, NIV®. Copyright © 1973, 1978, 1984, 2011 by Biblica, Inc.™ Used by permission of Zondervan. All rights reserved worldwide. www.zondervan.com The "NIV" and "New International Version" are trademarks registered in the United States Patent and Trademark Office by Biblica, Inc.™

NKJV: Scripture taken from the New King James Version. Copyright © 1982 by Thomas Nelson, Inc. Used by permission. All rights reserved.

NLT: Holy Bible, New Living Translation, copyright © 1996, 2004, 2015 by Tyndale House Foundation. Used by permission of Tyndale House Publishers, Inc. All rights reserved.

Cover design by Jessica Wei

ISBN: 978-1-68408-113-4

Contents

Introduction

The Bible is a book like no other. It is a gift from the Creator, a guidebook for life here on earth and a roadmap for life eternal. And it's a book of promises.

When God makes a promise, He keeps it. No exceptions. So the verses in this text are not hypotheticals; they're certainties. They apply to every generation, including yours, and they apply to every human being, including you.

Are you worried? Discouraged? Afraid? Trust the promises that God has made to you. Do you have a difficult task ahead? Ask your heavenly Father for courage. Do you have too many responsibilities and too little time to do them? Ask God to help you prioritize your day and your life. Whatever your circumstance, whatever your need, God is sufficient. No challenges are too big for Him, not even yours.

This book contains timeless promises and timely insights from notable women. The ideas on these pages are intended to remind you that the Lord is steadfast. Through the gift of grace, He offers eternal love and eternal life. It's a promise that you can depend on, now and forever.

1

Abundance

I have come that they may have life,
and that they may have it more abundantly.
JOHN 10:10 NKJV

God's abundance is available to each of us. He offers His blessings, but He doesn't force them upon us. To receive them, we must trust His promises and follow, as closely as we can, in the footsteps of His Son. But the world tempts us to do otherwise.

Everywhere you turn, someone or something is vying for your attention, trying to convince you that peace and happiness are commodities that can be purchased for the right price. But, buyer beware. Genuine peace and spiritual abundance are not for sale at any price. Real abundance is never obtained through worldly possessions. It results from your relationship with God.

Do you seek the abundant life that Jesus promises in John 10:10? Then turn your life and your heart over to Him. When you do, you'll receive the love, the peace, and the abundance that can only come from the touch of the Master's hand.

If you want purpose and meaning and satisfaction
and fulfillment and peace and hope and joy and
abundant life that lasts forever, look to Jesus.
ANNE GRAHAM LOTZ

God's Promises about Abundance

Until now you have asked for nothing
in My name. Ask and you will receive,
that your joy may be complete.
JOHN 16:24 HCSB

And God is able to make all grace abound to you,
so that always having all sufficiency in everything,
you may have an abundance for every good deed.
2 CORINTHIANS 9:8 NASB

Success, success to you, and success to those
who help you, for your God will help you.
1 CHRONICLES 12:18 NIV

My cup runs over. Surely goodness and mercy
shall follow me all the days of my life; and I will
dwell in the house of the LORD forever.
PSALM 23:5–6 NKJV

May Yahweh bless you and protect you;
may Yahweh make His face shine on you
and be gracious to you;
NUMBERS 6:24–25 HCSB

2

Acceptance

*Should we accept only good things
from the hand of God and never anything bad?*
JOB 2:10 NLT

All of us encounter situations and circumstances that we wish we could change but can't. Sometimes the problems are simply too big for us to solve. Sometimes the things we regret happened long ago, and no matter how many times we replay the events in our mind, the past remains unchanged. And sometimes we're swept up by life-altering events that we simply cannot control.

Reinhold Neibuhr penned a simple verse that has come to be known as the Serenity Prayer. It begins with a simple yet profound request: "God, grant me the serenity to accept the things I cannot change." Niebuhr's words are far easier to recite than they are to live by. Why? Because most of us want life to unfold in accordance with our own wishes and time-tables. But sometimes God has other plans.

If you've encountered unfortunate circumstances that are beyond your power to control, accept those circumstances. And trust God. When you do, you can be comforted in the knowledge that your Creator is good, that His love endures forever, and that He understands His plans perfectly, even when you do not.

*Acceptance says, "True, this is my situation
at the moment. I'll look unblinkingly at the reality
of it. But I'll also open my hands to accept willingly
whatever a loving Father sends."*
CATHERINE MARSHALL

God's Promises about Acceptance

*Everything God made is good, and nothing
should be refused if it is accepted with thanks.*
1 TIMOTHY 4:4 NCV

He is the LORD. He will do what He thinks is good.
1 SAMUEL 3:18 HCSB

*Trust in the LORD with all your heart
and lean not on your own understanding.*
PROVERBS 3:5 NIV

*For Yahweh is good, and His love is eternal;
His faithfulness endures through all generations.*
PSALM 100:5 HCSB

*For now we see in a mirror, dimly,
but then face to face. Now I know in part,
but then I shall know just as I also am known.*
1 CORINTHIANS 13:12 NKJV

3

Accepting Christ

For God so loved the world, that he gave his only
begotten Son, that whosoever believeth in him
should not perish, but have everlasting life.

JOHN 3:16 KJV

Jesus came to this world in order that each of us might live abundantly and eternally. He came so that our joy might be complete here on earth and, more importantly, in heaven. Christ loved us so much that He endured unspeakable pain on the cross so that we might be with Him throughout eternity.

How will you respond to Christ's sacrifice? Will you give Him your heart, your mind, and your soul? And will you accept the gift of eternal life, a gift that cost Him so much but can be yours for the asking? It's the most important decision you'll ever make. And if you choose wisely, it's a decision that you'll never regret.

Christ is the horn of our salvation,
the One who was secured on a cross so that we
could be secured in the Lamb's book of Life.

BETH MOORE

God's Promises about Accepting Christ

*And this is the testimony: God has given
us eternal life, and this life is in His Son.
The one who has the Son has life. The one who
doesn't have the Son of God does not have life.*

1 JOHN 5:11–12 HCSB

*For the wages of sin is death, but the gift of God
is eternal life in Christ Jesus our Lord.*

ROMANS 6:23 NIV

*The Spirit of God, who raised Jesus from the dead,
lives in you. And just as he raised Christ from
the dead, he will give life to your mortal bodies
by this same Spirit living within you.*

ROMANS 8:11 NLT

*Therefore we were buried with Him by baptism
into death, in order that, just as Christ was raised
from the dead by the glory of the Father,
so we too may walk in a new way of life.*

ROMANS 6:4 HCSB

*I am the good shepherd. The good shepherd
lays down his life for the sheep.*

JOHN 10:11 NIV

4

Adversity

We are hard-pressed on every side, yet not crushed;
we are perplexed, but not in despair.
2 CORINTHIANS 4:8 NKJV

Tough times. Disappointments. Hardship. Pain. These experiences are the inevitable cost that each of us must pay for being human. From time to time we all encounter adversity. Thankfully, we need never encounter it alone. God is always with us.

When we are troubled, God stands ready and willing to protect us. Our responsibility, of course, is to ask Him for protection. When we call upon Him in prayer, He will answer—in His own time and in His own way.

If you find yourself enduring difficult circumstances, remember that God remains in His heaven. If you become discouraged with the direction of your day or your life, turn your thoughts and prayers to Him. He is a God of possibility, not negativity. He will guide you through your difficulties and beyond them. And then, with a renewed spirit of optimism and hope, you can thank the Giver for gifts that are simply too numerous to count.

God will make obstacles serve His purpose.
LETTIE COWMAN

God's Promises about Adversity

I called to the LORD in my distress; I called to my God.
From His temple He heard my voice.
2 SAMUEL 22:7 HCSB

The LORD is my rock, my fortress,
and my deliverer, my God, my mountain
where I seek refuge. My shield, the horn
of my salvation, my stronghold,
my refuge, and my Savior.
2 SAMUEL 22:2–3 HCSB

God blesses those who patiently endure testing
and temptation. Afterward they will receive the crown
of life that God has promised to those who love him.
JAMES 1:12 NLT

He heals the brokenhearted
and binds up their wounds.
PSALM 147:3 HCSB

The LORD is my shepherd; I shall not want.
PSALM 23:1 KJV

5

Angels

*Do not neglect to show hospitality to strangers, for by
this some have entertained angels without knowing it.*
HEBREWS 13:2 NASB

The Bible promises that God sends angels to protect His children. He did so in Biblical times, and nothing has changed since then. Our beloved heavenly Father still sends emissaries to guide and protect His own.

Perhaps you don't spend much time contemplating the possibility that an angel might be nearby, serving the Creator while protecting you. Or maybe you've convinced yourself that God's angels have all gone into retirement. If so, think again. God is still at work, molding His universe and guiding His believers. And He's still using angels to help accomplish His plans.

*Even when we are frustrated by our inability
to understand a circumstance or event,
there are unseen angels bringing comfort
and protection as directed by God.*
MARY C. NEAL

God's Promises about Angels

*For the Son of man shall come in the glory
of his Father with his angels; and then he shall
reward every man according to his works.*
MATTHEW 16:27 KJV

*The harvest is the end of the age,
and the harvesters are angels.*
MATTHEW 13:39 HCSB

*For He will give His angels orders concerning you,
to protect you in all your ways.*
PSALM 91:11 HCSB

*Praise the LORD, you angels,
you mighty ones who carry out his plans,
listening for each of his commands.*
PSALM 103:20 NLT

*Are they not all ministering spirits, sent forth
to minister for them who shall be heirs of salvation?*
HEBREWS 1:14 KJV

6

Anger

*Everyone must be quick to hear, slow to speak,
and slow to anger, for man's anger does
not accomplish God's righteousness.*
JAMES 1:19–20 HCSB

The Bible promises that patience pays and anger costs. Anger is harmful, hurtful, and dangerous to your spiritual health. Whenever your thoughts are hijacked by angry emotions, you forfeit the peace and perspective that might otherwise be yours. And to make matters worse, angry thoughts may cause you to behave in irrational, self-destructive ways. As the old saying goes, "Anger is only one letter away from danger."

When we've been hurt badly, we don't forget easily. When we can identify the person who hurt us, we naturally focus our ire on the perpetrator. Unless we can find the inner strength to forgive that person, we're likely to internalize the anger for years, for decades, or for a lifetime. Anger turned inward is always detrimental to our spiritual health and disruptive to our lives. And that's one reason—but not the only reason—that we should learn how to forgive other people quickly and completely. To do otherwise will result in needless anger and inner turmoil.

First Peter 5:8–9 warns, "Stay alert! Watch out for

your great enemy, the devil. He prowls around like a roaring lion, looking for someone to devour. Stand firm against him, and be strong in your faith" (NLT). And of this you can be sure: Your adversary will use an unforgiving heart, and the inevitable anger that dwells within it, to sabotage your life and undermine your faith. To be safe, you must cleanse your heart, and you must forgive. You must say yes to God, yes to mercy, yes to love, and no to anger.

*It takes a lot of grace and maturity to simply forgive,
but a lot of healing takes place when you do.*
ELIZABETH GEORGE

God's Promises about Anger

*But I tell you that anyone who is angry
with a brother or sister will be subject to judgment.*
MATTHEW 5:22 NIV

*He who is slow to wrath has great understanding,
but he who is impulsive exalts folly.*
PROVERBS 14:29 NKJV

*A hot-tempered man stirs up conflict,
but a man slow to anger calms strife.*
PROVERBS 15:18 HCSB

7

Anxiety and Worry

Therefore do not worry about tomorrow,
for tomorrow will worry about its own things.
Sufficient for the day is its own trouble.

MATTHEW 6:34 NKJV

Because we are human beings who have the capacity to think and to anticipate future events, we worry. We worry about big things, little things, and just about everything in between. To make matters worse, we live in a world that breeds anxiety and fosters fear. So it's not surprising that when we come face to face with tough times, we may fall prey to discouragement, doubt, or depression. But our Father in heaven has other plans.

God has promised that we may lead lives of abundance, not anxiety. In fact, His Word instructs us to "be anxious for nothing." But how can we put our fears to rest? By taking those fears to Him and leaving them there.

The very same God who created the universe has promised to protect you now and forever. So what do you have to worry about? With God on your side, the answer is nothing.

Worry is like a rocking chair. It keeps you
moving but doesn't get you anywhere.

CORRIE TEN BOOM

God's Promises about Anxiety and Worry

Let not your heart be troubled;
you believe in God, believe also in Me.
JOHN 14:1 NKJV

Cast all your anxiety on him because he cares for you.
1 PETER 5:7 NIV

Peace I leave with you; My peace I give to you;
not as the world gives do I give to you. Do not let your
heart be troubled, nor let it be fearful.
JOHN 14:27 NASB

Do not be anxious about anything,
but in every situation, by prayer and petition,
with thanksgiving, present your requests to God.
PHILIPPIANS 4:6 NIV

Cast your burden on the LORD, and He shall sustain
you; He shall never permit the righteous to be moved.
PSALM 55:22 NKJV

8

Asking God

*Ask, and it will be given to you; seek, and you
will find; knock, and it will be opened to you.
For every one who asks receives, and he who seeks
finds, and to him who knocks it will be opened.*
MATTHEW 7:7–8 NASB

God invites us to ask Him for the things we need,
and He promises to hear our prayers as well as
our thoughts. The Lord is always available and He's
always ready to help us. And He knows precisely
what we need. But He still instructs us to ask.

Do you make a habit of asking God for the things
you need? Hopefully so. After all, the Father most
certainly has a plan for your life. And He can do great
things through you if you have the courage to ask for
His guidance and His help. So be fervent in prayer
and don't hesitate to ask the Creator for the tools you
need to accomplish His plan for your life. Then, get
busy and expect the best. When you do your part,
God will most certainly do His part. And great things
are bound to happen.

*God will help us become the people we are meant to be,
if only we will ask Him.*
HANNAH WHITALL SMITH

God's Promises about Asking Him

*Until now you have asked for nothing
in My name. Ask and you will receive,
that your joy may be complete.*
JOHN 16:24 HCSB

*Do not be anxious about anything,
but in everything, by prayer and petition,
with thanksgiving, present your requests to God.*
PHILIPPIANS 4:6 NIV

*The effective prayer of a righteous man
can accomplish much.*
JAMES 5:16 NASB

*Your Father knows the things
you have need of before you ask Him.*
MATTHEW 6:8 NKJV

*You did not choose me, but I chose you and appointed
you so that you might go and bear fruit—
fruit that will last—and so that whatever you
ask in my name the Father will give you.*
JOHN 15:16 NIV

9

Attitude

Finally, brothers, rejoice. Be restored,
be encouraged, be of the same mind, be at peace,
and the God of love and peace will be with you.
2 CORINTHIANS 13:11 HCSB

Attitudes are the mental filters through which we view and interpret the world around us. People with positive attitudes look for the best and usually find it. People burdened by chronically negative attitudes are not so fortunate.

Your attitude will inevitably determine the quality and direction of your day and your life. That's why it's so important to stay positive.

The Christian life can be, and should be, cause for celebration. After all, every new day is a gift, every new circumstance an opportunity to praise and to serve. So how will you direct your thoughts today? Will you focus on God's love? Will you hold fast to His promises and trust His plan for your life? Or will you allow your thoughts to be hijacked by negativity and doubt? If you're a thoughtful believer, you'll think optimistically about yourself and your future. And while you're at it, you'll give thanks to the Creator for more blessings than you can count.

*Developing a positive attitude means working
continually to find what is uplifting and encouraging.*
BARBARA JOHNSON

God's Promises about Attitude

A merry heart makes a cheerful countenance.
PROVERBS 15:13 NKJV

*You must have the same attitude
that Christ Jesus had.*
PHILIPPIANS 2:5 NLT

*Be glad and rejoice,
because your reward is great in heaven.*
MATTHEW 5:12 HCSB

Rejoice always; pray without ceasing.
1 THESSALONIANS 5:16–17 NASB

*This is the day the LORD has made;
let us rejoice and be glad in it.*
PSALM 118:24 HCSB

10

Beliefs

I have come as a light into the world, that whoever believes in Me should not abide in darkness.
JOHN 12:46 NKJV

Talking about our beliefs is easy; living by them is considerably harder. Yet God warns us that speaking about faith is not enough; we must also live by faith. Simply put, our theology must be demonstrated, not only with words but, more importantly, with actions.

As Christians, our instructions are clear: We should trust God's plan, obey God's Word, and follow God's Son. When we do these things, we inevitably partake in the spiritual abundance that the Creator has promised to those who walk in the light. But if we listen to God's instructions on Sunday morning but ignore them the rest of the week, we'll pay a heavy price for our misplaced priorities.

Every new day presents fresh opportunities to ensure that your actions are consistent with your beliefs. Seize those opportunities. Now.

Only believe, don't fear. Our Master, Jesus, always watches over us, and no matter what the persecution, Jesus will surely overcome it.
LOTTIE MOON

God's Promises about Beliefs

*Jesus said, "Because you have seen Me,
you have believed. Blessed are those
who believe without seeing."*
JOHN 20:29 HCSB

*I tell you the truth, whoever believes in me
will do the same things that I do. Those who
believe will do even greater things than these,
because I am going to the Father.*
JOHN 14:12 NCV

*Most assuredly, I say to you, he who believes in Me,
the works that I do he will do also.*
JOHN 14:12 NKJV

All things are possible for the one who believes.
MARK 9:23 NCV

*I know the One I have believed in
and am persuaded that He is able
to guard what has been
entrusted to me until that day.*
2 TIMOTHY 1:12 HCSB

11

The Bible

*For the word of God is living and effective and sharper
than any double-edged sword, penetrating as far
as the separation of soul and spirit, joints and marrow.
It is able to judge the ideas and thoughts of the heart.*

HEBREWS 4:12 HCSB

The promises found in God's Word are the cornerstone of the Christian faith. We must trust those promises and build our lives upon them.

The Bible is a priceless gift—a tool for Christians to use every day, in every situation. Yet too many Christians put away their spiritual toolkits and rely instead on the world's promises. Unfortunately, the world makes promises it doesn't keep. God has no such record of failure. He keeps every single one of His promises. On Him you can depend.

So how will you respond to God's promises? Will you treat your Bible as a one-of-a-kind guidebook for life here on earth and life eternal in heaven? Hopefully so because the Lord had given you all the tools you need to accomplish His plan for your life. He placed every instruction you'll need in the book He wrote. The rest is up to you.

*God's Word is a map you can safely follow
as you travel through life.*

ELIZABETH GEORGE

God's Promises about the Bible

All Scripture is given by inspiration of God,
and is profitable for doctrine, for reproof,
for correction, for instruction in righteousness.
2 TIMOTHY 3:16 KJV

Therefore everyone who hears these words
of mine and puts them into practice
is like a wise man who built his house on the rock.
MATHEW 7:24 NIV

Jesus answered, "It is written:
'Man shall not live on bread alone,
but on every word that comes
from the mouth of God.'"
MATTHEW 4:4 NIV

Your word is a lamp for my feet
and a light on my path.
PSALM 119:105 HCSB

12

Blessings

May Yahweh bless you and protect you;
may Yahweh make His face shine on you,
and be gracious to you.
NUMBERS 6:24–25 HCSB

If you tried to count all your blessings, how long would it take? A very, very long time. After all, you've been given the priceless gift of life here on earth and the promise of life eternal in heaven. And you've been given so much more.

Billy Graham noted: "We should think of the blessings we so easily take for granted: Life itself; preservation from danger; every bit of health we enjoy; every hour of liberty; the ability to see, to hear, to speak, to think, and to imagine all this comes from the hand of God." That's sound advice for believers—followers of the One from Galilee— who have so much to be thankful for.

Your blessings, all of which are gifts from above, are indeed too numerous to count, but it never hurts to begin counting them anyway. It never hurts to say thanks to the Giver for the gifts you can count, and all the other ones, too.

God is the giver, and we are the receivers.
And His richest gifts are bestowed not upon those
who do the greatest things, but upon those who
accept His abundance and His grace.

HANNAH WHITALL SMITH

God's Promises about Blessings

You will show me the path of life;
in Your presence is fullness of joy;
at Your right hand are pleasures forevermore.

PSALM 16:11 NKJV

The LORD is good to all:
and his tender mercies are over all his works.

PSALM 145:9 KJV

The LORD is my rock, my fortress,
and my deliverer, my God, my mountain where
I seek refuge. My shield, the horn of my salvation,
my stronghold, my refuge, and my Savior.

2 SAMUEL 22:2–3 HCSB

The LORD is my shepherd; I shall not want.

PSALM 23:1 KJV

Blessings crown the head of the righteous.

PROVERBS 10:6 NIV

13

Busyness

Return unto thy rest, O my soul;
for the LORD hath dealt bountifully with thee.
PSALM 116:7 KJV

For most of us, life is busy, perhaps too busy for our own good. We rush from place to place, with scarcely a moment to spare, checking smart phones along the way. Meanwhile, we're constantly bombarded by a steady stream of media, much of it disturbing. No wonder we're stressed!

Has the busy pace of twenty-first-century life robbed you of the peace and serenity that could otherwise be yours through Jesus Christ? If so, it's time to slow down, do less, and appreciate life a little more.

As you consider your priorities, remember that time with God is paramount. You owe it to yourself to spend time each day with your Creator, seeking His guidance and studying His Word. Those quiet moments of prayer and meditation are invaluable. When you let God help you organize your day, you'll find that He'll give you the time and the tools to do the most important tasks on your to-do list. And what about all those less important things on your list? Perhaps they're best left undone.

Strength is found not in busyness
and noise but in quietness.
LETTIE COWMAN

God's Promises about Busyness

Come unto me, all ye that labour
and are heavy laden, and I will give you rest.
MATTHEW 11:28 KJV

In quietness and in confidence
shall be your strength.
ISAIAH 30:15 KJV

Be still before the LORD
and wait patiently for Him.
PSALM 37:7 NIV

Rest in God alone, my soul,
for my hope comes from Him.
PSALM 62:5 HCSB

And the peace of God, which surpasses
all comprehension, will guard your hearts
and your minds in Christ Jesus.
PHILIPPIANS 4:7 NASB

14

Celebration

Rejoice in the Lord always.
Again I will say, rejoice!
PHILIPPIANS 4:4 NKJV

Each day contains cause for celebration. And each day has its own share of blessings. Our assignment, as grateful believers, is to look for the blessings and celebrate them.

Today, like every other day, is a priceless gift from God. He has offered us yet another opportunity to serve Him with smiling faces and willing hands. When we do our part, He inevitably does His part, and miracles happen.

The Lord has promised to bless you and keep you, now and forever. So, don't wait for birthdays or holidays. Make this day an exciting adventure. And while you're at it, take time to thank God for His blessings. He deserves your thanks, and you deserve the joy of expressing it.

Joy is the settled assurance that God is in control of all the details of my life, the quiet confidence that ultimately everything is going to be all right, and the determined choice to praise God in all things.
KAY WARREN

God's Promises about Celebration

A happy heart is like a continual feast.
PROVERBS 15:15 NCV

This is the day which the LORD has made;
let us rejoice and be glad in it.
PSALM 118:24 NASB

Rejoice always, pray without ceasing,
in everything give thanks; for this is the will of God
in Christ Jesus for you.
1 THESSALONIANS 5:16–18 NKJV

I delight greatly in the LORD;
my soul rejoices in my God.
ISAIAH 61:10 NIV

I came that they may have life,
and have it abundantly.
JOHN 10:10 NASB

15

Charity and Generosity

Freely you have received; freely give.
MATTHEW 10:8 NIV

The theme of generosity is woven into the fabric of God's Word. Our Creator instructs us to give generously—and cheerfully—to those in need. And He promises that when we do give of our time, our talents, and our resources, we will be blessed.

Jesus was the perfect example of generosity. He gave us everything, even His earthly life, so that we, His followers, might receive abundance, peace, and eternal life. He was always generous, always kind, always willing to help "the least of these." And, if we are to follow in His footsteps, we too must be generous.

Sometime today you'll encounter someone who needs a helping hand or a word of encouragement. When you encounter a person in need, think of yourself as Christ's ambassador. And remember that whatever you do for the least of these, you also do for Him.

*No matter how little you have,
you can always give some of it away.*
CATHERINE MARSHALL

God's Promises about Charity and Generosity

*So let each one give as he purposes in his heart,
not grudgingly or of necessity;
for God loves a cheerful giver.*
2 CORINTHIANS 9:7 NKJV

*You should remember the words of the Lord Jesus:
"It is more blessed to give than to receive."*
ACTS 20:35 NLT

*If you have two shirts, give one to the poor.
If you have food, share it with those who are hungry.*
LUKE 3:11 NLT

*Whenever we have the opportunity,
we should do good to everyone—
especially to those in the family of faith.*
GALATIANS 6:10 NLT

*Truly I tell you, whatever you did
for one of the least of these brothers
and sisters of mine, you did for me.*
MATTHEW 25:40 NIV

16

Cheerfulness

A cheerful heart has a continual feast.
PROVERBS 15:15 HCSB

As Christians, we have so many reasons to be cheerful: God is in His heaven; He remains firmly in control; He loves us; and through His Son He has offered us a path to eternal life. Despite these blessings, all of us will occasionally fall victim to the inevitable frustrations of everyday life. When we do, we should pause, take a deep breath, and remember how richly we've been blessed.

Cheerfulness is a gift that we give to others and to ourselves. The joy we give to others is reciprocal: whatever we give away is returned to us, oftentimes in greater measure. So make this promise to yourself and keep it: be a cheerful ambassador for Christ. He deserves no less, and neither, for that matter, do you.

How happy we are when we realize
that He is responsible, that He goes before,
that goodness and mercy shall follow us!
LETTIE COWMAN

God's Promises about Cheerfulness

Rejoice always, pray without ceasing,
in everything give thanks; for this
is the will of God in Christ Jesus for you.
1 THESSALONIANS 5:16–18 NKJV

This is the day that the LORD has made.
Let us rejoice and be glad today!
PSALM 118:24 NCV

Shout for joy to the LORD, all the earth.
Worship the LORD with gladness;
come before him with joyful songs.
PSALM 100:1–2 NIV

Do everything without grumbling and arguing,
so that you may be blameless and pure.
PHILIPPIANS 2:14–15 HCSB

A cheerful heart is good medicine,
but a crushed spirit dries up the bones.
PROVERBS 17:22 NIV

17

Christ's Love

As the Father loved Me,
I also have loved you; abide in My love.
JOHN 15:9 NKJV

Jesus loves us so much that He willingly sacrificed Himself on the cross so that we might live with Him throughout eternity. His love endures. Even when we falter, He loves us. When we fall prey to the world's temptations, He remains steadfast. In fact, no power on earth can separate us from His love.

Christ can transform us. When we open our hearts to Him and walk in His footsteps, our lives bear testimony to His mercy and to His grace. Yes, Christ's love changes everything. May we welcome Him into our hearts so that He can then change everything in us.

Jesus is all compassion.
He never betrays us.
CATHERINE MARSHALL

God's Promises about Christ's Love

*I am the good shepherd. The good shepherd
lays down his life for the sheep.*
JOHN 10:11 HCSB

*No one has greater love than this,
that someone would lay down his life for his friends.*
JOHN 15:13 HCSB

*For Christ also suffered once for sins,
the just for the unjust, that He might
bring us to God, being put to death
in the flesh but made alive by the Spirit.*
1 PETER 3:18 NKJV

We love him, because he first loved us.
1 JOHN 4:19 KJV

*For God so loved the world, that he gave
his only begotten Son, that whosoever believeth in him
should not perish, but have everlasting life.*
JOHN 3:16 KJV

18

Circumstances

Trust in him at all times, O people;
pour out your hearts to him, for God is our refuge.
PSALM 62:8 NIV

From time to time, all of us must endure unpleasant circumstances. We find ourselves in situations that we didn't ask for and probably don't deserve. During these times, we try our best to "hold up under the circumstances." But God has a better plan. He intends for us to rise *above* our circumstances, and He's promised to help us do it.

Are you dealing with a difficult situation or a tough problem? Do you struggle with occasional periods of discouragement and doubt? Are you worried, weary, or downcast? If so, don't face tough times alone. Face them with God as your partner, your protector, and your guide. When you do, He will give you the strength to meet any challenge, the courage to face any problem, and the patience to endure any circumstance.

The strength that we claim from God's Word
does not depend on circumstances. Circumstances
will be difficult, but our strength will be sufficient.
CORRIE TEN BOOM

God's Promises about Circumstances

*The Lord is a refuge for His people
and a stronghold.*
JOEL 3:16 NASB

*The Lord is a refuge for the oppressed,
a refuge in times of trouble.*
PSALM 9:9 HCSB

*Cast your burden on the Lord,
and He shall sustain you; He shall never
permit the righteous to be moved.*
PSALM 55:22 NKJV

*God is our protection and our strength.
He always helps in times of trouble.*
PSALM 46:1 NCV

*I have learned in whatever state I am,
to be content.*
PHILIPPIANS 4:11 NKJV

19

Comforting Others

Therefore, God's chosen ones, holy and loved,
put on heartfelt compassion, kindness,
humility, gentleness, and patience.
COLOSSIANS 3:12 HCSB

The world can be a dangerous and discouraging place, a place where real people experience real problems and real pain. When they do, we are presented with real opportunities to offer comfort. God wants us to seize those opportunities early and often.

Wherever you go, you'll encounter people who need your encouragement. Today, when you encounter someone who needs a comforting word, a pat on the back, a hug, or a helping hand, be quick to respond. You possess the power to make the world a better place one person at a time. When you use that power wisely, you make your own corner of the world a kinder, gentler, happier place.

God's Word instructs us to be kind and helpful, especially to those in need. So as you make your plans for the day ahead, look for people to comfort and people to help. When you do, you'll be a powerful example to others *and* a worthy servant to your Creator.

The measure of a life, after all,
is not its duration but its donation.
CORRIE TEN BOOM

God's Promises about Comforting Others

Let us think about each other and help
each other to show love and do good deeds.
HEBREWS 10:24 NCV

Do not withhold good from those to whom it is due,
when it is within your power to act.
PROVERBS 3:27 NIV

Do to others as you would have them do to you.
LUKE 6:31 NIV

So let's not get tired of doing what is good.
At just the right time we will reap
a harvest of blessing if we don't give up.
GALATIANS 6:9 NLT

Carry one another's burdens;
in this way you will fulfill the law of Christ.
GALATIANS 6:2 HCSB

20

Confidence

So we may boldly say: "The LORD is my helper;
I will not fear. What can man do to me?"
HEBREWS 13:6 NKJV

As Christians, we have every reason to live confidently. After all, we've read God's promises and
we know that He's prepared a place for us in heaven.
And with God on our side, what should we fear?
The answer, of course, is nothing. But sometimes,
despite our faith and despite God's promises, we find
ourselves gripped by earthly apprehensions.

When we focus on our doubts and fears, we can
concoct a lengthy list of reasons to lie awake at night
and fret about the uncertainties of the coming day.
A better strategy, of course, is to focus, not upon our
fears, but upon our God.

Are you a confident Christian? You should be.
God's promises never fail and His love is everlasting.
So the next time you need a boost of confidence, slow
down and have a little chat with your Creator. Count
your blessings, not your troubles. Focus on possibili-
ties, not problems. And remember that with God on
your side, you have absolutely nothing to fear.

Faith in God is the greatest power,
but great, too, is faith in oneself.
MARY MCLEOD BETHUNE

God's Promises about Confidence

You are my hope; O Lord God,
You are my confidence.
PSALM 71:5 NASB

I lift up my eyes to the mountains—
where does my help come from? My help comes
from the Lord, the Maker of heaven and earth.
PSALM 121:1-2 NIV

God is our refuge and strength,
a very present help in trouble.
PSALM 46:1 NKJV

Be strong and courageous, and do the work.
Don't be afraid or discouraged, for the Lord God,
my God, is with you. He won't leave you or forsake you.
1 CHRONICLES 28:20 HCSB

In this world you will have trouble.
But take heart! I have overcome the world.
JOHN 16:33 NIV

21

Contentment

I have learned in whatever state I am, to be content.
PHILIPPIANS 4:11 NKJV

The Bible promises that contentment can be ours if we honor God's commandments and follow, as closely as we can, in the footsteps of His Son. But the world seeks to sell you a different brand of contentment. The world promises that "happiness and serenity" can be purchased...at the right price. The world's marketers perpetuate the misconception that lasting satisfaction is for sale at the local mall, but nothing could be further from the truth. Genuine peace is not for sale at any price.

So where will you find contentment today? Will you trust God to provide it, or will you expect the world to do the job? If you expect the world to provide a sense of serenity and peace, you'll be disappointed sooner or later (probably sooner). But if you turn your heart and your life over to the One from Galilee, you'll be blessed now (and forever)...and you'll be content.

No matter what you're facing, embrace life in trust and contentment based on your faith in Jesus.
ELIZABETH GEORGE

God's Promises about Contentment

But godliness with contentment is a great gain.
1 TIMOTHY 6:6 HCSB

*Make sure that your character is free from
the love of money, being content with what you have;
for He Himself has said, "I will never desert you,
nor will I ever forsake you."*
HEBREWS 13:5 NASB

*A tranquil heart is life to the body,
but jealousy is rottenness to the bones.*
PROVERBS 14:30 HCSB

*Come unto me, all ye that labour
and are heavy laden, and I will give you rest.*
MATTHEW 11:28 KJV

*The peace of God, which passeth
all understanding, shall keep your hearts
and minds through Christ Jesus.*
PHILIPPIANS 4:7 KJV

22

Courage

Be strong and courageous, and do the work.
Do not be afraid or discouraged,
for the LORD God, my God, is with you.
1 CHRONICLES 28:20 NIV

As believers in a risen Christ, we can, and should, live courageously. After all, Jesus promises us that He has overcome the world and that He has made a place for us in heaven. So we have nothing to fear in the long term because our Lord will care for us throughout eternity. But what about those short-term, everyday worries that keep us up at night? And what about the life-altering hardships that leave us wondering if we can ever recover? The answer, of course, is that because God cares for us in good times and hard times, we can turn our concerns over to Him in prayer, knowing that all things ultimately work for the good of those who love Him.

When you form a one-on-one relationship with your Creator, you can be comforted by the fact that wherever you find yourself, whether at the top of the mountain or the depths of the valley, God is there with you. And because your Creator cares for you and protects you, you can rise above your fears.

At this very moment the Lord is seeking to work in you and through you. He's asking you to live

abundantly and courageously, and He's ready to help.
So why not let Him do it...starting now?

*Just as courage is faith in good, so discouragement
is faith in evil, and, while courage opens the door to
good, discouragement opens it to evil.*
HANNAH WHITALL SMITH

God's Promises about Courage

*Be on guard. Stand firm in the faith.
Be courageous. Be strong.*
1 CORINTHIANS 16:13 NLT

*For God has not given us a spirit of fearfulness,
but one of power, love, and sound judgment.*
2 TIMOTHY 1:7 HCSB

I can do all things through Him who strengthens me.
PHILIPPIANS 4:13 NASB

But He said to them, "It is I; do not be afraid."
JOHN 6:20 NKJV

*Behold, God is my salvation;
I will trust, and not be afraid.*
ISAIAH 12:2 KJV

23

Decisions

*But if any of you needs wisdom, you should
ask God for it. He is generous to everyone
and will give you wisdom without criticizing you.*
JAMES 1:5 NCV

Each day you must make countless decisions. Many of those decisions are so tightly woven into the fabric of your life that you scarcely realize that they are decisions at all. Other decisions are made purely out of habit. But occasionally you'll find yourself at one of life's inevitable crossroads, and when you do, it's time to slow down and have a heart-to-heart talk with the ultimate Counselor: your Father in heaven.

The Bible offers clear guidance about decision making. So if you're about to make an important decision, here are some things you can do:

1. Gather information. Don't expect to get all the facts—that's impossible—but try to gather as much information as you can in a reasonable amount of time (Proverbs 24:3–4).

2. Be patient. If you have time to make a decision, use that time to make a good decision (Proverbs 19:2).

3. Rely on the counsel of a few friends and

mentors. Proverbs 1:5 makes it clear: "A wise man will hear and increase learning, and a man of understanding will attain wise counsel." (NKJV).

4. Pray for guidance and listen carefully to your conscience.

5. When the time for action arrives, act. Procrastination is the enemy of progress; don't let it defeat you (James 1:22).

There may be no trumpet sound or loud applause when we make a right decision, just a calm sense of resolution and peace.
GLORIA GAITHER

God's Promises about Decisions

In every way be an example of doing good deeds. When you teach, do it with honesty and seriousness.
TITUS 2:7 NCV

We can make our own plans, but the LORD gives the right answer. People may be pure in their own eyes, but the LORD examines their motives.
PROVERBS 16:1–2 NLT

Blessed is the man who walks not in the counsel of the ungodly, nor stands in the path of sinners, nor sits in the seat of the scornful.
PSALM 1:1 NKJV

24

Devotions

*Morning by morning he wakens me and opens
my understanding to his will. The Sovereign L*ORD
has spoken to me, and I have listened.
ISAIAH 50:4-5 NLT

Every new day is a gift from the Creator, a gift that allows each of us to say "thank You" by spending time with the Giver. When we begin the day with our Bibles open and our hearts attuned to God, we are inevitably blessed by the promises we find in His Word.

Each day has 1,440 minutes. God deserves a few of those minutes. And you deserve the experience of spending a few quiet minutes with your Creator. So, if you haven't already done so, establish the habit of spending time with your Creator every day of the week. It's a habit that will change your day and revolutionize your life.

*Begin each day with God.
It will change your priorities.*
ELIZABETH GEORGE

God's Promises about Devotions

It is good to give thanks to the LORD,
And to sing praises to Your name, O Most High.
PSALM 92:1 NKJV

Heaven and earth will pass away,
but My words will never pass away.
MATTHEW 24:35 HCSB

Thy word is a lamp unto my feet,
and a light unto my path.
PSALM 119:105 KJV

Early the next morning, while it was still dark,
Jesus woke and left the house.
He went to a lonely place, where he prayed.
MARK 1:35 NCV

But grow in the grace and knowledge
of our Lord and Savior Jesus Christ. To Him be
the glory both now and to the day of eternity.
2 PETER 3:18 HCSB

25

Disappointments

*Then they cried out to the LORD in their trouble,
and He saved them out of their distresses.*
PSALM 107:13 NKJV

As we make the journey from the cradle to the grave, disappointments are inevitable. No matter how competent we are, no matter how fortunate, we still encounter circumstances that fall far short of our expectations. When tough times arrive, we have choices to make: we can feel sorry for ourselves, or we can get angry, or we can become depressed. Or, we can get busy praying about out problems and solving them.

When we are disheartened—on those cloudy days when our strength is sapped and our hope is shaken—there exists a source from which we can draw perspective and courage. That source is God. When we turn everything over to Him, we find that He is sufficient to meet our needs. No problem is too big for Him.

So, the next time you feel discouraged, slow down long enough to have a serious talk with your Creator. Pray for guidance, pray for strength, and pray for the wisdom to trust your heavenly Father. Your troubles are temporary; His love is not.

*Allow God to use the difficulties and disappointments
in life as polish to transform your faith into a glistening
diamond that takes in and reflects His love.*

ELIZABETH GEORGE

God's Promises about Disappointments

*He heals the brokenhearted
and binds up their wounds.*
PSALM 147:3 HCSB

*He shall not be afraid of evil tidings:
his heart is fixed, trusting in the LORD.*
PSALM 112:7 KJV

*Many adversities come to the one who is righteous,
but the LORD delivers him from them all.*
PSALM 34:19 HCSB

*My son, do not despise the chastening of the LORD,
nor be discouraged when you are rebuked by Him.*
HEBREWS 12:5 NKJV

They that sow in tears shall reap in joy.
PSALM 126:5 KJV

26

Dreams

When dreams come true, there is life and joy.
PROVERBS 13:12 NLT

Do you consider the future to be friend or foe? Do you expect the best, and are you willing to work for it? If so, please consider the fact that the Lord does, indeed, help those who help themselves. And He's especially helpful to those who consult Him before they finalize their plans.

God's help is always available to those who ask. Our job, of course, is to seek His guidance and His strength as we seek to accomplish His plans for our lives.

Nothing is too difficult for God, and no dreams are too big for Him—not even yours. When you do your part, He'll do His part, and great things are bound to happen. So live confidently, plan carefully, do your best, and leave the rest up to the Creator. You and He, working together, can move mountains. Lots of them.

When the dream of our heart is one that God
has planted there, a strange happiness flows into us.
At that moment, the spiritual resources
of the universe are released to help us.
CATHERINE MARSHALL

God's Promises about Dreams

Hope deferred makes the heart sick,
But when the desire comes, it is a tree of life.
PROVERBS 13:12 NKJV

Where there is no vision, the people perish.
PROVERBS 29:18 KJV

But we are hoping for something we do not have yet,
and we are waiting for it patiently.
ROMANS 8:25 NCV

Now may the God of hope fill you with all joy
and peace as you believe in Him, so that you may
overflow with hope by the power of the Holy Spirit.
ROMANS 15:13 HCSB

Humble yourselves therefore under the mighty hand
of God, that he may exalt you in due time.
1 PETER 5:6 KJV

27

Encouragement

But encourage each other daily,
while it is still called today, so that none of you
is hardened by sin's deception.
HEBREWS 3:13 HCSB

Whether we realize it or not, all of us need encouragement. The world can be a difficult place, a place where we encounter the inevitable disappointments that are woven into the fabric of everyday life. So we all need boosters who are ready, willing, and able to cheer us on when times get tough.

God's Word teaches that we must treat others as we ourselves wish to be treated. Since we desire encouragement for ourselves, we should be quick to share it with others.

Whom will you encourage today? How many times will you share a smile, or a kind word, or a pat on the back? You'll probably have many opportunities to share the gift of encouragement. When you seize those opportunities, others will be blessed, and you'll be blessed, too. But not necessarily in that order.

Developing a positive attitude means working
continually to find what is uplifting and encouraging.

BARBARA JOHNSON

God's Promises about Encouragement

*Let us think about each other and help each other
to show love and do good deeds.*
HEBREWS 10:24 ICB

*Bear one another's burdens,
and so fulfill the law of Christ.*
GALATIANS 6:2 NKJV

*So encourage each other and give each other strength,
just as you are doing now.*
1 THESSALONIANS 5:11 NCV

*When you talk, do not say harmful things,
but say what people need—words that will
help others become stronger. Then what you say
will do good to those who listen to you.*
EPHESIANS 4:29 NCV

*Now we exhort you, brethren, warn those
who are unruly, comfort the fainthearted,
uphold the weak, be patient with all.*
1 THESSALONIANS 5:14 NKJV

28

Enthusiasm

Whatever you do, do it enthusiastically,
as something done for the Lord and not for men.
COLOSSIANS 3:23 HCSB

As a woman who's striving to follow in the footsteps of God's Son, you have many reasons to be enthusiastic about your life, your opportunities, and your future. After all, your eternal destiny is secure. Christ died for your sins, and He wants you to experience life abundant and life eternal. So what's not to get excited about?

Are you a passionate person and an enthusiastic Christian? Are you genuinely excited about your faith, your family, and your future? Hopefully you can answer these questions with a resounding yes. But if your passion for life has waned, it's time to slow down long enough to recharge your spiritual batteries and reorder your priorities.

Each new day is an opportunity to put God first and celebrate His creation. Today, take time to count your blessings and take stock of your opportunities. And while you're at it, ask God for strength. When you sincerely petition Him, He will give you everything you need to live enthusiastically and abundantly.

The truth is that even in the midst of trouble,
happy moments swim by us every day,
like shining fish waiting to be caught.

BARBARA JOHNSON

God's Promises about Enthusiasm

Do your work with enthusiasm.
Work as if you were serving the Lord,
not as if you were serving only men and women.

EPHESIANS 6:7 NCV

A happy heart makes the face cheerful,
but heartache crushes the spirit.

PROVERBS 15:13 NIV

But as for me, I will hope continually,
and will praise You yet more and more.

PSALM 71:14 NASB

Rejoice always! Pray constantly.
Give thanks in everything,
for this is God's will for you in Christ Jesus.

1 THESSALONIANS 5:16–18 HCSB

Let the hearts of those who seek the LORD rejoice.
Look to the LORD and his strength; seek his face always.

1 CHRONICLES 16:10–11 NIV

29

Envy

Let us not be desirous of vainglory,
provoking one another, envying one another.
GALATIANS 5:26 KJV

God's Word warns us about a dangerous, destructive state of mind: envy. Envy is emotional poison. It poisons the mind and hardens the heart.

If we are to experience the abundant lives that Christ has promised, we must be on guard against the envious thoughts. Jealousy breeds discontent, discontent breeds unhappiness, and unhappiness robs us of the peace that might otherwise be ours.

So if the sin of envy has invaded your heart, ask God to help you heal. When you ask sincerely and often, He will respond. And when He does, you'll regain the peace that can only be found through Him.

The things we think are the things
that feed our souls. If we think on pure
and lovely things, we shall grow pure and lovely
like them; and the converse is equally true.
HANNAH WHITALL SMITH

God's Promises about Envy

So rid yourselves of all wickedness, all deceit,
hypocrisy, envy, and all slander.
1 PETER 2:1 HCSB

You must not covet your neighbor's house.
You must not covet your neighbor's wife,
male or female servant, ox or donkey,
or anything else that belongs to your neighbor.
EXODUS 20:17 NLT

Let us not become boastful,
challenging one another, envying one another.
GALATIANS 5:26 NASB

Where jealousy and selfishness are,
there will be confusion and every kind of evil.
JAMES 3:16 NCV

Don't envy evil men or desire to be with them.
PROVERBS 24:1 HCSB

30

Eternal Life

For God so loved the world, that he gave his only begotten Son, that whosoever believeth in him should not perish, but have everlasting life.

JOHN 3:16 KJV

Jesus is not only the light of the world; He is also its salvation. He came to this earth so that we might not perish but instead spend eternity with Him. What a glorious gift; what a priceless opportunity.

As mere mortals, we cannot fully understand the scope, and thus the value, of eternal life. Our vision is limited but God's is not. He sees all things; He knows all things; and His plans for you extend throughout eternity.

If you haven't already done so, this moment is the perfect moment to turn your life over to God's only begotten son. When you give your heart to the Son, you belong to the Father—today, tomorrow, and for all eternity.

Life is immortal, love eternal; death is nothing but a horizon, and a horizon is only the limit of our vision.

CORRIE TEN BOOM

God's Promises about Eternal Life

I assure you: Anyone who hears My word and believes
Him who sent Me has eternal life and will not come
under judgment but has passed from death to life.
JOHN 5:24 HCSB

For the wages of sin is death, but the gift of God
is eternal life in Christ Jesus our Lord.
ROMANS 6:23 NIV

I have written these things to you who believe
in the name of the Son of God, so that you
may know that you have eternal life.
1 JOHN 5:13 HCSB

The world and its desires pass away,
but whoever does the will of God lives forever.
1 JOHN 2:17 NIV

The last enemy that will be destroyed is death.
1 CORINTHIANS 15:26 NKJV

31

Faith

*For truly I say to you, if you have faith the size
of a mustard seed, you will say to this mountain,
"Move from here to there," and it will move;
and nothing will be impossible to you.*

MATTHEW 17:20 NASB

The Bible makes it clear: faith is powerful. With it, we can move mountains. With it, we can endure any hardship. With it, we can rise above the challenges of everyday life and live victoriously, whatever our circumstances.

Is your faith strong enough to move the mountains in your own life? If so, you're already tapped in to a source of strength that never fails: God's strength. But if your spiritual batteries are in need of recharging, don't be discouraged. God's strength is always available to those who seek.

The first element of a successful life is faith: faith in God, faith in His promises, and faith in His Son. When our faith in the Creator is strong, we can then have faith in ourselves, knowing that we are tools in the hands of a loving God who made mountains—and moves them—according to a perfect plan that only He can see.

I beg you to recognize the extreme simplicity of faith;
it is nothing more nor less than just believing God
when He says He either has done something for us,
or will do it; and then trusting Him to do it.
It is so simple that it is hard to explain.
HANNAH WHITALL SMITH

God's Promises about Faith

Don't be afraid, because I am your God.
I will make you strong and will help you;
I will support you with my right hand that saves you.
ISAIAH 41:10 NCV

Don't be afraid. Only believe.
MARK 5:36 HCSB

Blessed are they that have not seen,
and yet have believed.
JOHN 20:29 KJV

All things are possible for the one who believes.
MARK 9:23 NCV

And he said unto her, Daughter, thy faith
hath made thee whole; go in peace, and be whole.
MARK 5:34 KJV

32

Family

Choose for yourselves this day whom you will serve....
But as for me and my house, we will serve the LORD.
JOSHUA 24:15 NKJV

Our families are a gift from the Creator. God, in His infinite wisdom, has placed us precisely where we need to be to fulfill a plan that only He can see. Our families are a part of that plan, so we should be grateful, and we must never take our loved ones for granted.

When someone asked Mother Teresa how best to promote world peace, she said, "Go home and love your family." On another occasion, she observed, "Giving unselfishly to our own families tests the true heart of a servant of God."

Someone in your family probably needs help today. And everybody in your family needs love today. Or they need a word of encouragement. Or a pat on the back. Or a hug. Whether you realize it or not, the needs are great. And the next move is yours.

Line by line, moment by moment, special times
are etched into our memories in the permanent ink
of everlasting love in our relationships.
GLORIA GAITHER

God's Promises about Family

*Every kingdom divided against itself is headed for
destruction, and a house divided against itself falls.*
Luke 11:17 HCSB

*But if anyone does not provide for his own,
and especially for those of his household,
he has denied the faith and is worse than an unbeliever.*
1 Timothy 5:8 NASB

*Better a dry crust with peace
than a house full of feasting with strife.*
Proverbs 17:1 HCSB

*Their first responsibility is to show godliness
at home and repay their parents by taking care
of them. This is something that pleases God.*
1 Timothy 5:4 NLT

*But now faith, hope, love, abide these three;
but the greatest of these is love.*
1 Corinthians 13:13 NASB

33

Fear

*Peace I leave with you; My peace I give to you;
not as the world gives do I give to you.
Do not let your heart be troubled, nor let it be fearful.*
JOHN 14:27 NASB

From time to time, all of us experience difficult days when unexpected circumstances test our mettle. When these situations occur, fear creeps in and threatens to overtake our minds and our hearts.

Difficult times call for courageous measures. Running away from problems only perpetuates them; fear begets more fear; and anxiety is a poor counselor. As Maya Angelou observed, "Fear brings out the worst in everybody."

Adversity visits everyone—no human being is beyond Old Man Trouble's reach. But Old Man Trouble is not just an unwelcome guest, he is also an invaluable teacher. If we are to become mature human beings, it is our duty to learn from the inevitable hardships and heartbreaks of life.

Today, ask God to help you step beyond the boundaries of your fear. Ask Him to guide you to a place where you can realize your potential—a place where you are freed from the paralysis of anxiety. Ask Him to do His part, and then promise Him that you'll do your part. Don't ask God to lead you to a safe place; ask Him to lead you to the right place. And remember that those two places are seldom the same.

When fears regarding the cares of this world set in, we need to confidently lean on God's promise to care for us.
ELIZABETH GEORGE

God's Promises about Fear

But He said to them, "It is I; do not be afraid."
JOHN 6:20 NKJV

Fear not, for I am with you; be not dismayed, for I am your God. I will strengthen you, yes, I will help you, I will uphold you with My righteous right hand.
ISAIAH 41:10 NKJV

*The LORD is my light and my salvation—
whom should I fear?
The LORD is the stronghold of my life—
of whom should I be afraid?*
PSALM 27:1 HCSB

*Even though I walk through the darkest valley,
I will fear no evil, for you are with me;
your rod and your staff, they comfort me.*
PSALM 23:4 NIV

Be not afraid, only believe.
MARK 5:36 KJV

34

Following Christ

*Then He said to them all, "If anyone wants
to come with Me, he must deny himself,
take up his cross daily, and follow Me."*
Luke 9:23 HCSB

Every day, we're presented with countless opportunities to honor God by following in the footsteps of His Son. But we're sorely tempted to do otherwise. The world is filled to the brim with temptations and distractions that beckon us down a different path.

Elisabeth Elliot had this advice for believers everywhere: "Choose Jesus Christ! Deny yourself, take up the cross, and follow Him, for the world must be shown. The world must see, in us, a discernible, visible, startling difference."

Today, do your part to take up the cross and follow Him, even if the world encourages you to do otherwise. When you're traveling step-by-step with the Son of God, you're always on the right path.

*This my song through endless ages:
Jesus led me all the way.*
FANNY CROSBY

God's Promises about Following Christ

*But whoever keeps His word, truly in him
the love of God is perfected. This is how
we know we are in Him: the one who says
he remains in Him should walk just as He walked.*
1 JOHN 2:5-6 HCSB

*Walk in a manner worthy of the God
who calls you into His own kingdom and glory.*
1 THESSALONIANS 2:12 NASB

For we walk by faith, not by sight.
2 CORINTHIANS 5:7 HCSB

*Take my yoke upon you, and learn of me;
for I am meek and lowly in heart:
and ye shall find rest unto your souls.
For my yoke is easy, and my burden is light.*
MATTHEW 11:29-30 KJV

*Whoever is not willing to carry the cross and follow
me is not worthy of me. Those who try to hold on
to their lives will give up true life. Those who give up
their lives for me will hold on to true life.*
MATTHEW 10:38-39 NCV

35

Forgiveness

Judge not, and you shall not be judged.
Condemn not, and you shall not be condemned.
Forgive, and you will be forgiven.
LUKE 6:37 NKJV

For those who seek to follow in Christ's footsteps, forgiveness isn't optional; it's a commandment. Jesus didn't say, "Forgive when you feel like it," or "Forgive when it's easy." He instructed His followers to forgive quickly, completely, and repeatedly: "Then Peter came to Him and said, 'Lord, how often shall my brother sin against me, and I forgive him? Up to seven times?' Jesus said to him, 'I do not say to you, up to seven times, but up to seventy times seven'" (Matthew 18:21–22 NKJV).

Christ's instructions to Peter also apply to each of us. We are commanded—not encouraged, not advised; we are commanded—to forgive and to keep forgiving, even when it's hard.

Bitterness will consume your life if you let it. Hatred will rob you of peace. The search for revenge will leave you frustrated. The only peace that lasts is God's peace, which is only available to those who make the choice to forgive. Sometimes forgiveness is a hard choice to make, but the rewards are always worth the sacrifice.

Forgiveness is the key that unlocks the door
of resentment and the handcuffs of hate.
It is the power that breaks the chains of bitterness
and the shackles of selfishness.

CORRIE TEN BOOM

God's Promises about Forgiveness

But I say to you, love your enemies,
and pray for those who persecute you.

MATTHEW 5:44 NASB

And be kind to one another, tenderhearted,
forgiving one another, even as God in Christ forgave you.

EPHESIANS 4:32 NKJV

And whenever you stand praying, if you have anything
against anyone, forgive him, so that your Father
in heaven will also forgive you your wrongdoing.

MARK 11:25 HCSB

The merciful are blessed,
for they will be shown mercy.

MATTHEW 5:7 HCSB

36

Friends and Friendship

*A friend loves at all times,
and a brother is born for a time of adversity.*
PROVERBS 17:17 NIV

Our friends are gifts from above. God places them along our path and asks us to treat them with kindness, love, and respect. His Word teaches us that true friendship is a both a blessing and a treasure.

Emily Dickinson spoke for friends everywhere when she observed, "My friends are my estate." Dickinson understood that friends are among our most treasured possessions. But unlike a bank account or a stock certificate, the value of a true friendship is beyond measure.

Today, celebrate the joys of building and preserving your personal estate of lifelong friends. Give thanks for the laughter, the loyalty, the sharing, and the trust. And while you're at it, take the time to reconnect with a long-lost friend. When you do, you will have increased two personal fortunes at once.

*In friendship, God opens your eyes
to the glories of Himself.*
JONI EARECKSON TADA

God's Promises about Friends and Friendship

As iron sharpens iron,
so people can improve each other.
PROVERBS 27:17 NCV

Oil and incense bring joy to the heart,
and the sweetness of a friend
is better than self-counsel.
PROVERBS 27:9 HCSB

It is good and pleasant when God's people
live together in peace!
PSALM 133:1 NCV

Dear friends, if God loved us in this way,
we also must love one another.
1 JOHN 4:11 HCSB

Thine own friend, and thy father's friend,
forsake not.
PROVERBS 27:10 KJV

37

Gifts

Do not neglect the gift that is in you.
1 TIMOTHY 4:14 NKJV

God gives each of us special talents and opportunities. And He bestows these gifts for a reason: so that we might use them for His glory. But the world tempts us to do otherwise. Here in the twenty-first century, life is filled to the brim with distractions and temptations, each of which has the potential to distance us from the path God intends for us to take.

Do you possess financial resources? Share them. Do you have a spiritual gift? Share it. Do you have a personal testimony about the things that Christ has done for you? Tell your story. Do you possess a particular talent? Hone that skill and use it for God's glory.

All your talents, all your opportunities, and all your gifts are on temporary loan from the Creator. Use those gifts while you can because time is short and the needs are great. In every undertaking, make God your partner. Then, just as He promised, God will bless you now and forever.

*God has given you special gifts and talents—
now it's your turn to give them back to God.*
MARIE T. FREEMAN

God's Promises about Gifts

*God has given each of you a gift
from his great variety of spiritual gifts.
Use them well to serve one another.*
1 PETER 4:10 NLT

Now there are diversities of gifts, but the same Spirit.
1 CORINTHIANS 12:4 KJV

*Every good and perfect gift is from above,
coming down from the Father of the heavenly lights,
who does not change like shifting shadows.*
JAMES 1:17 NIV

*His master replied, "Well done, good and faithful
servant! You have been faithful with a few things;
I will put you in charge of many things.
Come and share your master's happiness!"*
MATTHEW 25:21 NIV

I remind you to fan into flame the gift of God.
2 TIMOTHY 1:6 NIV

38

God First

You shall have no other gods before Me.
EXODUS 20:3 NKJV

For most of us, these are very busy times. We have obligations at home, at work, at school, or on social media. From the moment we rise until we drift off to sleep at night, we have things to do and people to contact. So how do we find time for God? We must make time for Him, plain and simple. When we put God first, we're blessed. But when we succumb to the pressures and temptations of the world, we inevitably pay a price for our misguided priorities.

In the book of Exodus, God warns that we should put no gods before Him. Yet all too often, we place our Lord in second, third, or fourth place as we focus on other things. When we place our desires for possessions and status above our love for God—or when we yield to the countless distractions that surround us—we forfeit the peace that might otherwise be ours.

In the wilderness, Satan offered Jesus earthly power and unimaginable riches, but Jesus refused. Instead, He chose to worship His heavenly Father. We must do likewise by putting God first and worshiping Him only. God must come first. Always first.

*The most important thing you must decide
to do every day is put the Lord first.*
ELIZABETH GEORGE

God's Promises about Putting Him First

*Therefore, whether you eat or drink,
or whatever you do, do all to the glory of God.*
1 CORINTHIANS 10:31 NKJV

*For this is the love of God,
that we keep His commandments.
And His commandments are not burdensome.*
1 JOHN 5:3 NKJV

*How happy is everyone who fears the LORD,
who walks in His ways!*
PSALM 128:1 HCSB

*But prove yourselves doers of the word,
and not merely hearers who delude themselves.*
JAMES 1:22 NASB

We love him, because he first loved us.
1 JOHN 4:19 KJV

39

God's Calling

*I urge you to live a life worthy of the calling
you have received.*

EPHESIANS 4:1 NIV

God created you on purpose. He has a plan for
your life that only you, with your unique array of
talents and your own particular set of circumstances,
can fulfill. The Lord is calling you; He's gently guiding you to the place where you can accomplish the
greatest good for yourself and for His kingdom.

Have you already heard God's call? And are you
doing your best to pursue His plan for your life? If
so, you're blessed. But if you have not yet discovered
God's plan for your life, don't panic. There's still time
to hear His call and follow His path. To find that
path, keep searching and keep praying. Answers will
come— only one Creator has placed you in a particular
location, amid particular people, with unique opportunities to serve. And He has given you all the tools
you need to accomplish His plans. So listen for His
voice, watch for His signs, and prepare yourself for
the call—His call—that is certain to come.

*Only God's chosen task for you will ultimately satisfy.
Do not wait until it is too late to realize the privilege
of serving Him in His chosen position for you.*

BETH MOORE

God's Promises about His Calling

But as God has distributed to each one,
as the Lord has called each one, so let him walk.
1 CORINTHIANS 7:17 NKJV

And we know that all things work together
for good to those who love God, to those
who are the called according to His purpose.
ROMANS 8:28 NKJV

For whoever does the will of God
is My brother and My sister and mother.
MARK 3:35 NKJV

For many are called, but few are chosen.
MATTHEW 22:14 KJV

For you have need of endurance,
so that when you have done the will of God,
you may receive what was promised.
HEBREWS 10:36 NASB

40

God's Forgiveness

If we confess our sins, He is faithful
and righteous to forgive us our sins
and to cleanse us from all unrighteousness.
1 JOHN 1:9 NASB

The Bible promises us that God will forgive our sins if we ask Him. It's our duty to ask. When we've fulfilled that responsibility, He will always keep His promise. Yet many of us continue to punish ourselves—with needless guilt and self-loathing—for mistakes that our Creator has long since forgiven and forgotten (Isaiah 43:25).

If you haven't managed to forgive yourself for some past mistake, or for a series of poor decisions, it's time to rearrange your thinking. If God has forgiven you, how can you withhold forgiveness from yourself? The answer, of course, is that God's mercy is intended to wash your sins away. That's what the Lord wants, and if you're good enough for Him, you're good enough.

We cannot out-sin God's ability to forgive us.
BETH MOORE

God's Promises about His Forgiveness

*All the prophets testify about Him
that through His name everyone who
believes in Him will receive forgiveness of sins.*
Acts 10:43 HCSB

*Let us, then, feel very sure that we can come before
God's throne where there is grace. There we can
receive mercy and grace to help us when we need it.*
Hebrews 4:16 NCV

*But the mercy of the Lord is from everlasting
to everlasting upon them that fear him,
and his righteousness unto children's children.*
Psalm 103:17 KJV

Be merciful, just as your Father is merciful.
Luke 6:36 NIV

*It is I who sweep away your transgressions
for My own sake and remember your sins no more.*
Isaiah 43:25 HCSB

41

God's Guidance

*Trust in the LORD with all your heart, and lean not
on your own understanding; in all your ways
acknowledge Him, and He shall direct your paths.*

PROVERBS 3:5–6 NKJV

When we ask for God's guidance, with our hearts
and minds open to His direction, He will lead
us along a path of His choosing. But for many of us,
listening to God is hard. We have so many things we
want, and so many needs to pray for, that we spend
far more time talking at God than we do listening to
Him.

Corrie ten Boom observed, "God's guidance
is even more important than common sense. I can
declare that the deepest darkness is outshone by the
light of Jesus." These words remind us that life is
best lived when we seek the Lord's direction early
and often.

Our Father has many ways to make Himself
known. Our challenge is to make ourselves open to
His instruction. So, if you're unsure of your next step,
trust God's promises and talk to Him often. When
you do, He'll guide your steps today, tomorrow,
and forever.

*God's guidance is even more important
than common sense. I can declare that the deepest
darkness is outshone by the light of Jesus.*

CORRIE TEN BOOM

God's Promises about His Guidance

*Yet LORD, You are our Father; we are the clay, and You
are our potter; we all are the work of Your hands.*

ISAIAH 64:8 HCSB

*The LORD says, "I will guide you along
the best pathway for your life.
I will advise you and watch over you."*

PSALM 32:8 NLT

*Teach me to do Your will, for You are my God;
Your Spirit is good. Lead me in the land of uprightness.*

PSALM 143:10 NKJV

*Shew me thy ways, O LORD; teach me thy paths.
Lead me in thy truth, and teach me: for thou art
the God of my salvation; on thee do I wait all the day.*

PSALM 25:4–5 KJV

*Morning by morning he wakens me and opens
my understanding to his will. The Sovereign LORD
has spoken to me, and I have listened.*

ISAIAH 50:4–5 NLT

42

God's Love

*And we have known and believed the love
that God has for us. God is love, and he who abides
in love abides in God, and God in him.*
1 JOHN 4:16 NKJV

God's love is infinite. His love spans the entirety of His creation. His love touches the far reaches of His vast universe as well as the quiet corners of every human heart.

Sometimes, amid the crush of everyday life, God may seem very far away. He is not. God is always with us, night and day; He never leaves us, even for a moment. When we earnestly seek Him, we will find Him because He is always right here, waiting patiently for us to reach out to Him. Our job, of course, is to reach out to Him.

*Nothing can separate you from God's love,
absolutely nothing. God is enough for time,
God is enough for eternity. God is enough!*
HANNAH WHITALL SMITH

God's Promises about His Love

We love him, because he first loved us.
1 JOHN 4:19 KJV

Let us, then, feel very sure that we can come before
God's throne where there is grace. There we can
receive mercy and grace to help us when we need it.
HEBREWS 4:16 NCV

But the mercy of the LORD is from everlasting
to everlasting upon them that fear him,
and his righteousness unto children's children....
PSALM 103:17 KJV

Be merciful, just as your Father is merciful.
LUKE 6:36 NIV

It is I who sweep away your transgressions
for My own sake and remember your sins no more.
ISAIAH 43:25 HCSB

43

God's Plan

*But as it is written: What eye did not see and ear did
not hear, and what never entered the human mind—
God prepared this for those who love Him.*

1 CORINTHIANS 2:9 HCSB

God has a plan for this world and for your world.
It's a plan that He understands perfectly, a plan
that can bring you untold joy now and throughout
eternity. But the Lord won't force His plan upon you.
He's given you free will, the ability to make choices
on your own. The totality of those choices will determine how well you fulfill God's calling.

Sometimes God makes Himself known in obvious
ways, but more often His guidance is subtle. So we
must be quiet to hear His voice.

If you're serious about discovering God's plan for
your life—or rediscovering it—start spending quiet
time with Him every day. Ask Him for direction. Pray
for clarity. And be watchful for His signs. The more
time you spend with Him, the sooner the answers
will come.

*Often God has to shut a door in our face
so that He can subsequently open the door
through which He wants us to go.*
CATHERINE MARSHALL

God's Promises about His Plan

For My thoughts are not your thoughts,
and your ways are not My ways.... For as heaven
is higher than earth, so My ways are higher
than your ways, and My thoughts than your thoughts.
ISAIAH 55:8–9 HCSB

And yet, O LORD, you are our Father.
We are the clay, and you are the potter.
We are all formed by your hand.
ISAIAH 64:8 NLT

For whoever does the will of God
is My brother and My sister and mother.
MARK 3:35 NKJV

It is God who is at work in you,
both to will and to work for His good pleasure.
PHILIPPIANS 2:13 NASB

We must do the works of Him who sent Me
while it is day. Night is coming when no one can work.
JOHN 9:4 HCSB

44

God's Presence

*For the eyes of Yahweh roam throughout
the earth to show Himself strong for those
whose hearts are completely His.*
2 CHRONICLES 16:9 HCSB

God is everywhere: everywhere you've ever been, everywhere you'll ever be. He is not absent from our world, nor is He absent from your world. God is not "out there"; He is "right here," continuously reshaping His universe and continuously reshaping the lives of those who dwell in it.

Your Creator is with you always, listening to your thoughts and prayers, watching over your every move. If the demands of everyday life weigh down upon you, you may be tempted to ignore God's presence or—worse yet—lose faith in His promises. But when you quiet yourself and acknowledge His presence, God will touch your heart and renew your strength.

Psalm 46:10 remind us to "Be still, and know that I am God" (NIV). When we do, we can be comforted in the knowledge that God does not love us from a distance. He is not just near. He is here.

To experience joy on a daily basis,
learn what it means to live in the moment.
Living in the moment helps us recognize
that God can be found in this moment,
whether it contains joy or sorrow.
KAY WARREN

God's Promises about His Presence

Be still, and know that I am God.
PSALM 46:10 KJV

Draw near to God, and He will draw near to you.
JAMES 4:8 HCSB

I know the LORD is always with me.
I will not be shaken, for he is right beside me.
PSALM 16:8 NLT

Though I walk through the valley of the shadow
of death, I will fear no evil: for thou art with me.
PSALM 23:4 KJV

I am not alone, because the Father is with Me.
JOHN 16:32 NKJV

45

God's Promises

*Let us hold on to the confession of our hope
without wavering, for He who promised is faithful.*
HEBREWS 10:23 HCSB

The Bible contains promises upon which you, as a believer, can depend. When the Creator of the universe makes a pledge to you, He will keep it. No exceptions.

You can think of the Bible as a written contract between you and your heavenly Father. When you fulfill your obligations to Him, the Lord will most certainly fulfill His covenant to you.

When we accept Christ into our hearts, God promises us the opportunity to experience contentment, peace, and spiritual abundance. But more importantly, God promises that the priceless gift of eternal life will be ours. These promises should give us comfort. With God on our side, we have absolutely *nothing* to fear in this world and *everything* to hope for in the next

*Gather the riches of God's promises.
Nobody can take away from you those texts
from the Bible which you have learned by heart.*
CORRIE TEN BOOM

God's Promises

Sustain me as You promised, and I will live;
do not let me be ashamed of my hope.
PSALM 119:116 HCSB

As for God, his way is perfect:
the word of the LORD is tried:
he is a buckler to all those that trust in him.
PSALM 18:30 KJV

They will bind themselves to the LORD
with an eternal covenant
that will never again be broken.
JEREMIAH 50:5 NLT

My God is my rock, in whom I take refuge,
my shield and the horn of my salvation.
2 SAMUEL 22:2–3 NIV

He heeded their prayer,
because they put their trust in Him.
1 CHRONICLES 5:20 NKJV

46

God's Support

Nevertheless God, who comforts
the downcast, comforted us.
2 CORINTHIANS 7:6 NKJV

God's Word promises that He will support you in good times and comfort you in hard times. The Creator of the universe stands ready to give you the strength to meet any challenge and the courage to face any adversity. When you ask for God's help, He responds in His own way and at His own appointed hour. But make no mistake: He always responds.

In a world brimming with dangers and temptations, God is the ultimate armor. In a world saturated with misleading messages, God's Word is the ultimate truth. In a world filled with frustrations and distractions, God's Son offers the ultimate peace.

Today, as you encounter the inevitable challenges of everyday life, remember that your heavenly Father never leaves you, not even for a moment. He's always available, always ready to listen, always ready to lead. When you make a habit of talking to Him early and often, He'll guide you and comfort you every day of your life.

God's all-sufficiency is a major. Your inability
is a minor. Major in majors, not in minors.
CORRIE TEN BOOM

God's Promises about His Support

My grace is sufficient for you,
for my power is made perfect in weakness.
2 CORINTHIANS 12:9 NIV

Therefore, we may boldly say: The Lord is my helper;
I will not be afraid. What can man do to me?
HEBREWS 13:6 HCSB

Therefore humble yourselves under the mighty
hand of God, that He may exalt you in due time,
casting all your care upon Him, for He cares for you.
1 PETER 5:6–7 NKJV

The LORD is my light and my salvation—
whom should I fear? The LORD
is the stronghold of my life—
of whom should I be afraid?
PSALM 27:1 HCSB

The LORD is my shepherd; I shall not want.
He makes me to lie down in green pastures;
He leads me beside the still waters.
He restores my soul.
PSALM 23:1–3 NKJV

47

Grace

But because of his great love for us, God,
who is rich in mercy, made us alive with Christ
even when we were dead in transgressions—
it is by grace you have been saved.
EPHESIANS 2:4-5 NIV

God's grace is sufficient to meet our every need. No matter our circumstances, no matter our personal histories, the Lord's precious gifts are always available. All we need do is form a personal, life-altering relationship with His only begotten Son, and we're secure, now and forever.

Grace is unearned, undeserved favor from God. His grace is available to each of us. No sin is too terrible, no behavior too outrageous, to separate us from God's love. We are saved by grace *through faith*. Jesus paid for our sins on the cross, and when we trust Him completely, God pronounces us "not guilty" of our transgressions.

Have you accepted Christ as your King, your Shepherd, and your Savior? If so, you are protected now and forever. If not, this moment is the appropriate time to trust God's Son and accept God's grace. It's never too soon, or too late, to welcome Jesus into your heart.

*How beautiful it is to learn that grace
isn't fragile, and that in the family of God
we can fail and not be a failure.*

GLORIA GAITHER

God's Promises about Grace

*But grow in the grace and knowledge of our Lord
and Savior Jesus Christ. To Him be the glory,
both now and to the day of eternity.*

2 PETER 3:18 NASB

*We have redemption in Him through His blood,
the forgiveness of our trespasses, according
to the riches of His grace that He lavished
on us with all wisdom and understanding.*

EPHESIANS 1:7–8 HCSB

*My grace is sufficient for you, for my power
is made perfect in weakness.*

2 CORINTHIANS 12:9 NIV

*But he gives us more grace. That is why
Scripture says: "God opposes the proud
but gives grace to the humble."*

JAMES 4:6 NIV

*For by grace you have been saved through faith,
and that not of yourselves; it is the gift of God,
not of works, lest anyone should boast.*

EPHESIANS 2:8–9 NKJV

48

Happiness

Those who listen to instruction will prosper;
those who trust the LORD will be joyful.
PROVERBS 16:20 NLT

Everywhere we turn, or so it seems, the message is clear: happiness is for sale, and if we have enough money, we can buy it. But God's Word contains a different message. In the Bible, we are taught that happiness is a byproduct, the result of living in harmony with God's plan for our lives. Obedience is the path to peace, love, and happiness. Disobedience is the path to discouragement, dissatisfaction, and doubt.

Happiness also depends on the way we think. If we form the habit of focusing on the positive aspects of life, we tend to be happier. But if we choose to dwell on the negatives, our very own thoughts have the power to make us miserable.

Do you want to be a happy Christian? Then you must start by being an obedient Christian. Then you must set your mind and heart upon God's blessings. When you think about it, you have many reasons to be joyful. When you count your blessings every day—and obey your Creator—you'll discover that happiness is not a commodity to be purchased; it is, instead, the natural consequence of walking daily with God.

When we bring sunshine into the lives of others,
we're warmed by it ourselves. When we spill
a little happiness, it splashes on us.
BARBARA JOHNSON

God's Promises about Happiness

If they obey and serve him, they will spend
the rest of their days in prosperity
and their years in contentment.
JOB 36:11 NIV

I have come that they may have life,
and that they may have it more abundantly.
JOHN 10:10 NKJV

Happiness makes a person smile,
but sadness can break a person's spirit.
PROVERBS 15:13 NCV

A joyful heart is good medicine,
but a broken spirit dries up the bones.
PROVERBS 17:22 HCSB

Joyful is the person who finds wisdom,
the one who gains understanding.
PROVERBS 3:13 NLT

49

Helping Others

Carry one another's burdens;
in this way you will fulfill the law of Christ.
GALATIANS 6:2 HCSB

If you're looking for somebody to help, you won't have to look very far. Somebody very close needs a helping hand, or a hot meal, or a pat on the back, or a prayer. In order to find that person, you'll need to keep your eyes and your heart open, and you'll need to stay focused on the needs of others. Focusing, however, is not as simple as it seems.

We live in a fast-paced, media-driven world filled with countless temptations and time-wasting distractions. Sometimes we may convince ourselves that we simply don't have the time or the resources to offer help to the needy. Such thoughts are misguided. Caring for our neighbors must be *our* priority because it is *God's* priority.

God has a specific plan for your life, and part of that plan involves service to His children. Service is not a burden; it's an opportunity. Seize your opportunity today. Tomorrow may be too late.

It is one of the most beautiful compensations
of life that no one can sincerely try to help
another without helping herself.
BARBARA JOHNSON

God's Promises about Helping Others

Let us not become weary in doing good,
for at the proper time we will reap
a harvest if we do not give up.
GALATIANS 6:9 NIV

Whenever you are able,
do good to people who need help.
PROVERBS 3:27 NCV

If you have two shirts, give one to the poor.
If you have food, share it with those who are hungry.
LUKE 3:11 NLT

Whatever you did for one of the least
of these brothers of Mine, you did for Me.
MATTHEW 25:40 HCSB

Therefore, as we have opportunity, we must work
for the good of all, especially for those
who belong to the household of faith.
GALATIANS 6:10 HCSB

50

Hope

*Let us hold fast the confession of our hope
without wavering, for He who promised is faithful.*

HEBREWS 10:23 NASB

God's promises give up hope: hope for today, hope
for tomorrow, hope for all eternity. The hope that
the world offers is temporary, at best. But the hope
that God offers never grows old and never goes out
of date. It's no wonder, then, that when we pin our
hopes on worldly resources, we are often disappointed.
Thankfully, God has no such record of failure.

The Bible teaches that the Lord blesses those who
trust in His wisdom and follow in the footsteps of His
Son. Will you count yourself among that number?
When you do, you'll have every reason on earth—and
in heaven—to be hopeful about your future. After all,
God has made important promises to you, promises
that He is certainly going to keep. So be hopeful, be
optimistic, be faithful, and do your best. Then, leave
the rest up to God. Your destiny is safe with Him.

*Never yield to gloomy anticipation. Place your hope
and confidence in God. He has no record of failure.*

LETTIE COWMAN

God's Promises about Hope

This hope we have as an anchor of the soul,
a hope both sure and steadfast.
HEBREWS 6:19 NASB

I say to myself, "The LORD is mine,
so I hope in him."
LAMENTATIONS 3:24 NCV

The LORD is good to those who wait for Him,
to the soul who seeks Him.
It is good that one should hope
and wait quietly for the salvation of the LORD.
LAMENTATIONS 3:25–26 NKJV

Hope deferred makes the heart sick,
But when the desire comes, it is a tree of life.
PROVERBS 13:12 NKJV

Be strong and courageous,
all you who put your hope in the Lord.
PSALM 31:24 HCSB

51

Joy

This is the day which the Lord has made;
let us rejoice and be glad in it.
PSALM 118:24 NASB

The joy that the world offers is fleeting and incomplete: here today, gone tomorrow, not coming back anytime soon. But God's joy is different. His joy has staying power. In fact, it's a gift that never stops giving to those who welcome His Son into their hearts.

Psalm 100 reminds us to celebrate the lives that God has given us: "Shout for joy to the Lord, all the earth. Worship the Lord with gladness; come before Him with joyful songs." (v. 1–2 NIV). Yet sometimes, amid the inevitable complications and predicaments that are woven into the fabric of everyday life, we forget to rejoice. Instead of celebrating life, we complain about it. This is an understandable mistake, but a mistake nonetheless. As Christians, we are called by our Creator to live joyfully and abundantly. To do otherwise is to squander His spiritual gifts.

This day and every day, Christ offers you His peace and His joy. Accept it and share it with others, just as He has shared His joy with you.

Joy is the keynote of the Christian life.
It is not something that happens. It is a gift,
given to us in the coming of Christ.
ELISABETH ELLIOT

God's Promises about Joy

Rejoice in the Lord always. Again I will say, rejoice!
PHILIPPIANS 4:4 NKJV

Rejoice always, pray without ceasing,
in everything give thanks; for this is the will
of God in Christ Jesus for you.
1 THESSALONIANS 5:16–18 NKJV

I have spoken these things to you so that My joy
may be in you and your joy may be complete.
JOHN 15:11 HCSB

Until now you have asked for nothing
in My name. Ask and you will receive,
so that your joy may be complete.
JOHN 16:24 HCSB

So you also have sorrow now.
But I will see you again. Your hearts will rejoice,
and no one will rob you of your joy.
JOHN 16:22 HCSB

52

Judging Others

Judge not, and you shall not be judged.
Condemn not, and you shall not be condemned.
Forgive, and you will be forgiven.
LUKE 6:37 NKJV

The need to judge others seems to be woven into the very fabric of human consciousness. We mortals feel compelled to serve as informal judges and juries, pronouncing our own verdicts on the actions and perceived motivations of others, all the while excusing—or oftentimes hiding—our own shortcomings. But God's Word instructs us to let Him be the judge. He knows that we, with our limited knowledge and personal biases, are simply ill-equipped to assess the actions of others. The act of judging, then, becomes not only an act of futility, but also an affront to our Creator.

When Jesus came upon a woman who had been condemned by the Pharisees, He spoke not only to the people who had gathered there, but also to all generations. Christ warned, "He that is without sin among you, let him first cast a stone at her" (John 8:7 KJV). The message is clear: because we are all sinners, we must refrain from the temptation to judge others.

So the next time you're tempted to cast judgment

on another human being, resist that temptation. God hasn't called you to be a judge; He's called you to be a witness.

> *Don't judge other people more harshly than you want God to judge you.*
> MARIE T. FREEMAN

God's Promises about Judging Others

Don't criticize one another, brothers. He who criticizes a brother or judges his brother criticizes the law and judges the law. But if you judge the law, you are not a doer of the law but a judge.
JAMES 4:11 HCSB

Therefore, any one of you who judges is without excuse. For when you judge another, you condemn yourself, since you, the judge, do the same things.
ROMANS 2:1 HCSB

Do everything without grumbling and arguing, so that you may be blameless and pure.
PHILIPPIANS 2:14–15 HCSB

Those who guard their lips preserve their lives, but those who speak rashly will come to ruin.
PROVERBS 13:3 NIV

53

Kindness and Compassion

Therefore, whatever you want men to do to you,
do also to them, for this is the Law and the Prophets.
MATTHEW 7:12 NKJV

Jesus set the example: He was compassionate, loving, and kind. If we seek to follow Him, we, too, must combine compassionate hearts with willing hands.

John Wesley said: "Do all the good you can. By all the means you can. In all the ways you can. In all the places you can. At all the times you can. To all the people you can. As long as ever you can." His advice still applies. In order to follow in Christ's footsteps, we must be compassionate. There is simply no other way.

Never underestimate the power of kindness. You never know when a kind word or gesture might significantly improve someone's day, or week, or life. So be quick to offer words of encouragement, and smiles, and pats on the back. Be generous with your resources and your time. Make kindness the cornerstone of your dealings with others. They will be blessed, and you will be, too. And everybody wins.

When we bring sunshine into the lives of others,
we're warmed by it ourselves. When we spill
a little happiness, it splashes on us.
BARBARA JOHNSON

God's Promises about Kindness and Compassion

A new commandment I give unto you,
that ye love one another; as I have loved you,
that ye also love one another.
JOHN 13:34 KJV

Who is wise and has understanding among you?
He should show his works by good conduct
with wisdom's gentleness.
JAMES 3:13 HCSB

Be kind to one another, tender-hearted,
forgiving each other, just as God in Christ
also has forgiven you.
EPHESIANS 4:32 NASB

And let us not grow weary while doing good,
for in due season we shall reap if we do not lose heart.
GALATIANS 6:9 NKJV

Assuredly, I say to you, inasmuch as you did it to one
of the least of these My brethren, you did it to Me.
MATTHEW 25:40 NKJV

54

Love

And now abide faith, hope, love, these three;
but the greatest of these is love.
1 CORINTHIANS 13:13 NKJV

God is love, and He intends that we share His love with the world. But He won't force us to be loving and kind. He places that responsibility squarely on our shoulders.

Love, like everything else in this world, begins and ends with God, but the middle part belongs to us. The Creator gives each of us the opportunity to be kind, to be courteous, and to be loving. He gives each of us the chance to obey the Golden Rule, or to make up our own rules as we go. If we obey God's instructions, we're secure, but if we do otherwise, we suffer.

Christ's words are clear: "'Love the Lord your God with all your heart and with all your soul and with all your mind.' This is the first and greatest commandment. And the second is like it: 'Love your neighbor as yourself.' All the Law and the Prophets hang on these two commandments" (Matthew 22:37–40 NIV). We are commanded to love the One who first loved us and then to share His love with the world. And the next move is always ours.

The vast ocean of Love cannot be measured
or explained, but it can be experienced.
SARAH YOUNG

God's Promises about Love

A new commandment I give unto you,
that ye love one another; as I have loved you,
that ye also love one another.
JOHN 13:34 KJV

Love is patient, love is kind. Love does not envy,
is not boastful, is not conceited.
1 CORINTHIANS 13:4 HCSB

Beloved, if God so loved us,
we ought also to love one another.
1 JOHN 4:11 KJV

Above all, love each other deeply,
because love covers a multitude of sins.
1 PETER 4:8 NIV

And we have known and believed the love that God
has for us. God is love, and he who abides in love
abides in God, and God in him.
1 JOHN 4:16 NKJV

55

Materialism

*No one can serve two masters. For you will hate
one and love the other; you will be devoted
to one and despise the other. You cannot serve
both God and be enslaved to money.*

LUKE 16:13 NLT

The world's message is abundantly clear: collect
enough material possessions and you'll be
happy. But God's Word warns against such shallow
thinking. The Bible teaches us that the love of
money—and the love of things that money can buy—
is a trap that inevitably leads to disappointment, to
disillusionment, and, ultimately, to destruction.

On the grand stage of a well-lived life, material
possessions should play a rather small role. Of course,
we all need the basic necessities of life, but once we
meet those needs for ourselves and for our families,
the piling up of possessions creates more problems
than it solves. Our real riches, of course, are not of
this world. We are never really rich until we are rich
in spirit.

So, if you're a woman who finds herself wrapped
up in the concerns of the material world, it's time to
reorder your priorities. And it's time to begin storing
up riches that will endure throughout eternity—the
spiritual kind.

*It's sobering to contemplate how much time,
effort, sacrifice, compromise, and attention we give
to acquiring and increasing our supply of something
that is totally insignificant in eternity.*

ANNE GRAHAM LOTZ

God's Promises about Materialism

*For where your treasure is,
there your heart will be also.*

LUKE 12:34 HCSB

*Your life should be free from the love of money.
Be satisfied with what you have, for He Himself
has said, I will never leave you or forsake you.*

HEBREWS 13:5 HCSB

*We brought nothing into the world,
so we can take nothing out. But, if we have food
and clothes, we will be satisfied with that.*

1 TIMOTHY 6:7–8 NCV

*Do not love the world or the things that belong
to the world. If anyone loves the world,
love for the Father is not in him.*

1 JOHN 2:15 HCSB

*There is one who makes himself rich, yet has nothing;
and one who makes himself poor, yet has great riches.*

PROVERBS 13:7 NKJV

56

Miracles

Is anything too hard for the LORD?
GENESIS 18:14 NKJV

God's power has no limitations. He is not restrained by the laws of nature because He created those laws. At any time, at any place, under any set of circumstances, He can accomplish anything He chooses. The things that seem miraculous to us are, to Him, expressions of His power and His love.

Do you expect God to work miracles in your own life? You should. From the moment He created our universe out of nothingness, the Lord has made a habit of doing miraculous things. And He's still working miracles today.

With God nothing is impossible. His wondrous works come in all shapes and sizes, so keep your eyes and your heart open. Somewhere, a miracle is about to happen, and it might just happen to *you*.

*It is wonderful what miracles God works
in wills that are utterly surrendered to Him.*
HANNAH WHITALL SMITH

God's Promises about Miracles

*God confirmed the message by giving signs
and wonders and various miracles and by giving
gifts of the Holy Spirit whenever he chose.*
HEBREWS 2:4 NLT

*What no eye has seen, what no ear has heard,
and what no human mind has conceived—
the things God has prepared for those who love him.*
1 CORINTHIANS 2:9 NIV

*You are the God of great wonders!
You demonstrate your awesome power
among the nations.*
PSALM 77:14 NLT

*And Jesus looking upon them saith,
With men it is impossible, but not with God:
for with God all things are possible.*
MARK 10:27 KJV

For with God nothing shall be impossible.
LUKE 1:37 KJV

57

Obedience

Now by this we know that we know Him,
if we keep His commandments.
1 JOHN 2:3 NKJV

God's instructions to mankind are contained in a book like no other: the Holy Bible. When we obey God's commandments and listen carefully to the conscience He has placed in our hearts, we are secure. But if we disobey our Creator, if we choose to ignore the teachings and the warnings of His Word, we do so at great peril.

Susanna Wesley said, "There are two things to do about the gospel: believe it and behave it." Her words serve as a powerful reminder that, as Christians, we are called to take God's promises seriously and to live in accordance with His teachings.

God gave us His commandments for a reason: so that we might obey them and be blessed. Yet we live in a world that presents us with countless temptations to stray far from His path. It is our responsibility to resist those temptations with vigor. Obedience isn't just the best way to experience the full measure of God's blessings; it's the only way.

When we are obedient,
God guides our steps and our stops.
CORRIE TEN BOOM

God's Promises about Obedience

We must obey God rather than men.
ACTS 5:29 NASB

Teach me, O LORD, the way of Thy statutes,
and I shall observe it to the end.
PSALM 119:33 NASB

Trust in the LORD with all your heart, and lean not
on your own understanding; in all your ways
acknowledge Him, and He shall direct your paths.
PROVERBS 3:5–6 NKJV

Praise the LORD! Happy are those who respect
the LORD, who want what he commands.
PSALM 112:1 NCV

But prove yourselves doers of the word,
and not merely hearers who delude themselves.
JAMES 1:22 NASB

58

Past

*Do not remember the former things, nor consider
the things of old. Behold, I will do a new thing.*
ISAIAH 43:18–19 NKJV

Since we can't change the pains and disappointments of the past, why do so many of us insist
upon replaying them over and over again in our
minds? Perhaps it's because we can't find it in our
hearts to forgive the people who have hurt us. Being
mere mortals, we seek revenge, not reconciliation,
and we harbor hatred in our hearts, sometimes for
decades.

Reinhold Niebuhr composed a simple verse that
came to be known as the Serenity Prayer: "God, grant
me the serenity to accept the things I cannot change,
the courage to change the things I can, and the wisdom to know the difference." Obviously, we cannot
change the past. It is what it was and forever will be.
The present, of course, is a different matter.

Today is filled with opportunities to live, to love,
to work, to play, and to celebrate life. If we sincerely
wish to build a better tomorrow, we can start building it today, in the present moment. So, if you've
endured a difficult past, accept it, learn from it, and
forgive everybody, including yourself. Once you've
made peace with your past, don't spend too much

time there. Instead, live in the precious present, where opportunities abound and change is still possible.

We set our eyes on the finish line,
forgetting the past, and straining toward the mark
of spiritual maturity and fruitfulness.
VONETTE BRIGHT

God's Promises about the Past

One thing I do, forgetting those things which
are behind and reaching forward to those things
which are ahead, I press toward the goal for
the prize of the upward call of God in Christ Jesus.
PHILIPPIANS 3:13–14 NKJV

Have mercy on me, O God, according to your
unfailing love; according to your great compassion
blot out my transgressions. Wash away all my
iniquity and cleanse me from my sin.
PSALM 51:1–2 NIV

Your old sinful self has died,
and your new life is kept with Christ in God.
COLOSSIANS 3:3 NCV

He restoreth my soul: he leadeth me in the paths
of righteousness for his name's sake.
PSALM 23:3 KJV

59

Patience

A person's wisdom yields patience;
it is to one's glory to overlook an offense.
PROVERBS 19:11 NIV

Time and again, the Bible promises us that patience is its own reward, but not its only reward. Yet we human beings are, by nature, an impatient lot. We know what we want and we know when we want it: right now!

We live in an imperfect world inhabited by imperfect family members, imperfect friends, imperfect acquaintances, and imperfect strangers. Sometimes we inherit troubles from these imperfect people, and sometimes we create troubles for ourselves. In either case, what's required is patience: patience for other people's shortcomings as well as our own.

Proverbs 16:32 teaches, "Better to be patient than powerful; better to have self-control than to conquer a city" (NLT). But for most of us, waiting patiently is hard. We are fallible beings who want things today, not tomorrow. Still, God instructs us to be patient and that's what we must do. It's the peaceful way to live.

The times we find ourselves having to wait
on others may be the perfect opportunities
to train ourselves to wait on the Lord.

JONI EARECKSON TADA

God's Promises about Patience

Patience of spirit is better than haughtiness of spirit.

ECCLESIASTES 7:8 NASB

Better to be patient than powerful;
better to have self-control than to conquer a city.

PROVERBS 16:32 NLT

But if we hope for what we do not yet have,
we wait for it patiently.

ROMANS 8:25 NIV

Be joyful in hope, patient in affliction,
faithful in prayer.

ROMANS 12:12 NIV

The LORD is good to those who depend on him,
to those who search for him. So it is good to wait
quietly for salvation from the LORD.

LAMENTATIONS 3:25–26 NLT

60

Peace

*Peace I leave with you, My peace I give to you;
not as the world gives do I give to you. Let not
your heart be troubled, neither let it be afraid.*

JOHN 14:27 NKJV

Peace. It's such a beautiful word. It conveys images
of serenity, contentment, and freedom from the
trials and tribulations of everyday existence. Peace
means freedom from conflict, freedom from inner
turmoil, and freedom from worry. Peace is such a
beautiful concept that advertisers and marketers
attempt to sell it with images of relaxed vacation-
ers lounging on the beach or happy senior citizens
celebrating on the golf course. But contrary to the
implied claims of modern media, real peace, genuine
peace, isn't for sale. At any price.

Have you discovered the genuine peace that can
be yours through Christ? Or are you still scurrying
after the illusion of peace that the world promises
but cannot deliver? If you've turned things over to
Jesus, you'll be blessed now and forever. So what are
you waiting for? Let Him rule your heart and your
thoughts, beginning now. When you do, you'll experience the peace that only He can give.

Peace does not mean to be in a place where
there is no noise, trouble, or hard work.
Peace means to be in the midst of all those
things and still be calm in your heart.

CATHERINE MARSHALL

God's Promises about Peace

He Himself is our peace.

EPHESIANS 2:14 NASB

The peace of God, which passeth
all understanding, shall keep your
hearts and minds through Christ Jesus.

PHILIPPIANS 4:7 KJV

But the fruit of the Spirit is love, joy, peace, patience,
kindness, goodness, faith, gentleness, self-control.
Against such things there is no law.

GALATIANS 5:22–23 HCSB

"I will give peace, real peace, to those far and near,
and I will heal them," says the LORD.

ISAIAH 57:19 NCV

These things I have spoken to you, that in Me you may
have peace. In the world you will have tribulation;
but be of good cheer, I have overcome the world.

JOHN 16:33 NKJV

61

Perseverance

Let us not become weary in doing good,
for at the proper time we will
reap a harvest if we do not give up.
GALATIANS 6:9 NIV

Occasionally, good things happen with little or no effort. Somebody wins the lottery, or inherits a fortune, or stumbles onto a financial bonanza by being at the right place at the right time. But more often than not, good things happen to people who work hard, and keep working hard, when just about everybody else has gone home or given up.

Christina Rossetti said, "A fall is not a signal to lie wallowing, but to rise." And St. Catherine of Siena observed, "Nothing great was ever done without much enduring." Both women were right. Perseverance pays.

Every marathon has a finish line, and so does yours. So keep putting one foot in front of the other, pray for strength, and don't give up. Whether you realize it or not, you're up to the challenge if you persevere. And with God's help, that's exactly what you'll do.

We are all on our way somewhere.
We'll get there if we just keep going.
BARBARA JOHNSON

God's Promises about Perseverance

But as for you, be strong; don't be discouraged,
for your work has a reward.
2 Chronicles 15:7 HCSB

We are hard-pressed on every side, yet not crushed;
we are perplexed, but not in despair.
2 Corinthians 4:8 NKJV

Finishing is better than starting.
Patience is better than pride.
Ecclesiastes 7:8 NLT

For you have need of endurance,
so that when you have done the will of God,
you may receive what was promised.
Hebrews 10:36 NASB

So let us run the race that is before us
and never give up. We should remove from
our lives anything that would get in the way
and the sin that so easily holds us back.
Hebrews 12:1 NCV

62

Praise

Let everything that breathes praise the LORD. Hallelujah!
PSALM 150:6 HCSB

Time and again, God's Word teaches that it pays to praise our Creator. God doesn't need our praise, nor does He require it before He dispenses His blessings. But we need the experience of praising Him, and He smiles upon us when we do.

When we consider God's blessings and the sacrifices of His Son, just how thankful should we be? Should we praise our Creator once a day? Are two prayers enough? Is it sufficient that we praise our heavenly Father at mealtimes and bedtimes? The answer, of course, is no. When we consider how richly we have been blessed, now and forever—and when we consider the price Christ paid on the cross—it becomes clear that we should offer many prayers of thanks throughout the day.

Our lives expand or contract in proportion to our gratitude. When we are appropriately grateful for God's countless blessings, we experience His peace. But if we ignore His gifts, we invite stress, anxiety, and sadness into our lives. So, throughout this day, pause and say silent prayers of thanks. When you do, you'll discover that a grateful heart reaps countless blessings that a hardened heart will never know.

This is my story, this is my song,
praising my Savior, all the day long.
FANNY CROSBY

God's Promises about Praise

Great is the LORD! He is most worthy of praise!
No one can measure his greatness.
PSALM 145:3 NLT

In everything give thanks;
for this is the will of God in Christ Jesus for you.
1 THESSALONIANS 5:18 NKJV

At the name of Jesus every knee should bow,
of things in heaven, and things in earth,
and things under the earth; and that every tongue
should confess that Jesus Christ is Lord,
to the glory of God the Father.
PHILIPPIANS 2:10–11 KJV

The LORD is my strength and my song;
He has become my salvation.
EXODUS 15:2 HCSB

From the rising of the sun to its setting,
the name of the LORD is to be praised.
PSALM 113:3 NASB

63

Prayer

*Rejoice always, pray without ceasing,
in everything give thanks; for this is the
will of God in Christ Jesus for you.*
1 THESSALONIANS 5:16–18 NKJV

Prayer is a powerful tool that you can use to change your world and change yourself. God hears every prayer and responds in His own way and according to His own timetable. When you make a habit of consulting Him about everything, He'll guide you along a path of His choosing, which, by the way, is the path you should take. And when you petition Him for strength, He'll give you the courage to face any problem and the power to meet any challenge.

So today, instead of turning things over in your mind, turn them over to God in prayer. Take your concerns to the Lord and leave them there. Your heavenly Father is listening, and He wants to hear from you. Now.

*Don't pray when you feel like it.
Have an appointment with the Lord and keep it.*
CORRIE TEN BOOM

God's Promises about Prayer

I desire therefore that the men pray everywhere,
lifting up holy hands, without wrath and doubting.
1 TIMOTHY 2:8 NKJV

Is anyone among you suffering? He should pray.
JAMES 5:13 HCSB

Confess your trespasses to one another, and pray for
one another, that you may be healed. The effective,
fervent prayer of a righteous man avails much.
JAMES 5:16 NKJV

And whenever you stand praying,
if you have anything against anyone,
forgive him, so that your Father in heaven
may also forgive you your wrongdoing.
MARK 11:25 HCSB

Ask, and it will be given to you; seek, and you
will find; knock, and it will be opened to you.
For every one who asks receives, and he who seeks
finds, and to him who knocks it will be opened.
MATTHEW 7:7-8 NASB

64

Purpose

*We have also received an inheritance in Him,
predestined according to the purpose of the One
who works out everything in agreement
with the decision of His will.*
EPHESIANS 1:11 HCSB

God doesn't do things by accident. He didn't put you here by chance. The Lord didn't deliver you to your particular place, at this particular time, with your particular set of talents and opportunities on a whim. He has a plan, a one-of-a-kind mission designed especially for you. Discovering that plan may take time. But if you keep asking God for guidance, He'll lead along a path of His choosing and give you every tool you need to fulfill His will.

Of course, you'll probably encounter a few impediments as you attempt to discover the exact nature of God's purpose for your life. And you may travel down a few dead ends along the way. But if you keep searching, and if you genuinely seek the Lord's guidance, He'll reveal His plans at a time and place of His own choosing.

Today and every day, God is beckoning you to hear His voice and follow His plan for your life. When you listen—and when you answer His call—

you'll be amazed at the wonderful things that an all-knowing, all-powerful God can do.

When God gives you a mission, He also gives you everything you need to fulfill that mission.
ELIZABETH GEORGE

God's Promises about Purpose

So whether you eat or drink, or whatever you do, do it all for the glory of God.
1 CORINTHIANS 10:31 NLT

For we are God's co-workers. You are God's field, God's building.
1 CORINTHIANS 3:9 HCSB

For we are His creation, created in Christ Jesus for good works, which God prepared ahead of time so that we should walk in them.
EPHESIANS 2:10 HCSB

We must do the works of Him who sent Me while it is day. Night is coming when no one can work.
JOHN 9:4 HCSB

And whatever you do, do it heartily, as to the Lord and not to men.
COLOSSIANS 3:23 NKJV

65

Quiet Time

*Now in the morning, having risen a long while
before daylight, He went out and departed
to a solitary place; and there He prayed.*
MARK 1:35 NKJV

Jesus understood the importance of silence. He spent precious hours alone with God, and so should we. But with our busy schedules, we're tempted to rush from place to place, checking smart phones along the way, leaving no time to contemplate spiritual matters.

You live in a noisy world, a complicated society where sights and sounds surround you and silence is in short supply. Everywhere you turn, or so it seems, the media seeks to grab your attention and hijack your thoughts. You're surrounded by big screens and little ones. And your phone can keep you logged in day and night if you let it. Don't let it.

Today and every day, you need quiet, uninterrupted time alone with God. You need to be still and listen for His voice. And you need to seek His guidance in matters great and small. Your Creator has important plans for your day and your life. And He's trying to get His message through. You owe it to Him—and to yourself—to listen and to learn *in silence.*

It is in that stillness that the Voice will be heard,
the only voice in all the universe that speaks
peace to the deepest part of us.
ELISABETH ELLIOT

God's Promises about Quiet Time

Truly my soul silently waits for God;
from Him comes my salvation.
PSALM 62:1 NKJV

Be still, and know that I am God.
PSALM 46:10 KJV

Listen in silence before me.
ISAIAH 41:1 NLT

In quietness and in confidence
shall be your strength.
ISAIAH 30:15 KJV

To everything there is a season...
a time to keep silence, and a time to speak.
ECCLESIASTES 3:1, 7 KJV

66

Renewal

Therefore, if anyone is in Christ,
he is a new creation; old things have passed away;
behold, all things have become new.
2 CORINTHIANS 5:17 NKJV

For busy citizens of the twenty-first century, it's easy to become overcommitted, overworked, and over-stressed. If we choose, we can be connected 24-7, sparing just enough time to a few hours' sleep each night. What we need is time to renew and re-charge, but where can we find the time? We can—and should—find it with God.

God can renew your strength and restore your spirits if you let Him. But He won't force you to slow down, and He won't insist that you get enough sleep at night. He leaves those choices up to you.

If you're feeling chronically tired or discouraged, it's time to rearrange your schedule, turn off the TV, power down the phone, and spend quiet time with your Creator. He knows what you need, and He wants you to experience His peace and His love. He's ready, willing, and perfectly able to renew your strength and help you prioritize the items on your do-list if you ask Him. In fact, He's ready to hear your prayers right now. Please don't make Him wait.

God's power is great enough for our deepest desperation. You can go on. You can pick up the pieces and start anew. You can face your fears. You can find peace in the rubble. There is healing for your soul.

Suzanne Dale Ezell

God's Promises about Renewal

You are being renewed in the spirit of your minds; you put on the new self, the one created according to God's likeness in righteousness and purity of the truth.

Ephesians 4:23–24 HCSB

Those who hope in the Lord will renew their strength. They will soar on wings like eagles; they will run and not grow weary, they will walk and not be faint.

Isaiah 40:31 NIV

Remember ye not the former things, neither consider the things of old. Behold, I will do a new thing.

Isaiah 43:18–19 KJV

Finally, brothers, rejoice. Be restored, be encouraged, be of the same mind, be at peace, and the God of love and peace will be with you.

2 Corinthians 13:11 HCSB

67

Service and Serving God

The greatest among you will be your servant.
For those who exalt themselves will be humbled,
and those who humble themselves will be exalted.
MATTHEW 23:11–12 NIV

How do we achieve greatness in the eyes of God? By accumulating wealth? By acquiring power? By gaining fame, popularity, or prestige? Of course not. We achieve greatness in God's eyes by serving His children gladly, humbly, and often.

Everywhere we look, the needs are great. Whether here at home or halfway around the globe, so many people are enduring difficult circumstances. They need help, and as Christians, we are instructed to serve them.

Jesus came to this world, not to conquer but to serve. We must do likewise by helping those who cannot help themselves. When we do, our lives will be blessed by the One who first served us.

What is needed for happy effectual service is simply to put your work into the Lord's hand, and leave it there.
HANNAH WHITALL SMITH

God's Promises about Serving Him

*Shepherd God's flock, for whom you
are responsible. Watch over them because you want to,
not because you are forced. That is how God wants it.
Do it because you are happy to serve.*
1 PETER 5:2 NCV

*As each one has received a gift,
minister it to one another, as good stewards
of the manifold grace of God.*
1 PETER 4:10 NKJV

*Blessed are those servants, whom the lord
when he cometh shall find watching.*
LUKE 12:37 KJV

*Assuredly, I say to you, inasmuch as you did it to one
of the least of these My brethren, you did it to Me.*
MATTHEW 25:40 NKJV

*Even so faith, if it hath not works,
is dead, being alone.*
JAMES 2:17 KJV

68

Spiritual Growth

*I remind you to fan into flames
the spiritual gift God gave you.*
2 TIMOTHY 1:6 NLT

As a Christian, you should never stop growing. No matter your age, no matter your circumstances, you have opportunities to learn and opportunities to serve. Wherever you happen to be, God is there, too, and He wants to bless you with an expanding array of spiritual gifts. Your job is to let Him.

The path to spiritual maturity unfolds day by day. Through prayer, through Bible study, and through obedience to God's Word, we can strengthen our relationship with Him. The more we focus on the Father, the more He blesses our lives.

In the quiet moments when we open our hearts to the Lord, the Creator who made us keeps remaking us. He gives us guidance, perspective, courage, and strength. And the appropriate moment to accept these spiritual gifts is always the present one.

*Spiritual growth doesn't happen automatically
and is rarely pretty; we will all be
"under construction" until the day we die and we
finally take hold of the "life that is truly life."*
KAY WARREN

God's Promises about Spiritual Growth

But endurance must do its complete work,
so that you may be mature
and complete, lacking nothing.
JAMES 1:4 HCSB

But grow in the grace and knowledge
of our Lord and Savior Jesus Christ.
To Him be the glory both now and forever. Amen.
2 PETER 3:18 NKJV

And be not conformed to this world:
but be ye transformed by the renewing of your mind,
that ye may prove what is that good,
and acceptable, and perfect, will of God.
ROMANS 12:2 KJV

Leave inexperience behind, and you will live;
pursue the way of understanding.
PROVERBS 9:6 HCSB

So let us stop going over the basics of Christianity
again and again. Let us go on instead
and become mature in our understanding.
HEBREWS 6:1 NLT

69

Strength

He gives strength to the weary,
and to him who lacks might He increases power.
ISAIAH 40:29 NASB

When you're weary or worried, where do you turn for strength? The medicine cabinet? The gym? The health food store? The spa? These places may offer a temporary energy boost, but the best place to turn for strength and solace isn't down the hall or at the mall; it's as near as your next breath. The best source of strength is God.

God's love for you never changes, and neither does His support. From the cradle to the grave, He has promised to give you the strength to meet the challenges of life. He has promised to guide you and protect you if you let Him. But He also expects you to do your part.

Today provides yet another opportunity to partake in the strength that only God can provide. You do so by attuning your heart to Him through prayer, obedience, and trust. Life can be challenging, but fear not. Whatever your challenge, God can give you the strength to face it and overcome it. Let Him.

*The strength that we claim from God's Word
does not depend on circumstances. Circumstances
will be difficult, but our strength will be sufficient.*

CORRIE TEN BOOM

God's Promises about Strength

*The Lord is my strength and my song;
He has become my salvation.*

EXODUS 15:2 HCSB

*My grace is sufficient for you,
for my power is made perfect in weakness.*

2 CORINTHIANS 12:9 NIV

*Have faith in the Lord your God,
and you will stand strong. Have faith in his prophets,
and you will succeed.*

2 CHRONICLES 20:20 NCV

*Be strong and courageous, and do the work.
Don't be afraid or discouraged, for the Lord God,
my God, is with you. He won't leave you or forsake you.*

1 CHRONICLES 28:20 HCSB

I can do all things through Christ who strengthens me.

PHILIPPIANS 4:13 NKJV

70

Thanksgiving

Enter into His gates with thanksgiving,
and into His courts with praise. Be thankful to Him,
and bless His name. For the LORD is good; His mercy
is everlasting, and His truth endures to all generations.
PSALM 100:4–5 NKJV

Each of us has much to be thankful for. We all have more blessings than we can count, beginning with the precious gift of life. Every good gift comes from our Father above, and we owe Him our never-ending thanks. But sometimes, when the demands of everyday life press down upon us, we neglect to express our gratitude to the Creator.

God loves us and cares for us; He has a plan for each of us; and He has offered us the gift of eternal life through His Son. Considering all the things that the Lord has done, we owe it to Him—and to ourselves—to slow down many times each day and offer our thanks. His grace is everlasting; our thanks should be, too.

Fill up the spare moments of your life
with praise and thanksgiving.
SARAH YOUNG

God's Promises about Thanksgiving

And whatever you do, in word or in deed,
do everything in the name of the Lord Jesus,
giving thanks to God the Father through Him.

COLOSSIANS 3:17 HCSB

Rejoice always, pray without ceasing,
in everything give thanks; for this is the will of God
in Christ Jesus for you.

1 THESSALONIANS 5:16–18 NKJV

Surely the righteous shall give thanks to Your name;
the upright shall dwell in Your presence.

PSALM 140:13 NKJV

I will thank Yahweh with all my heart;
I will declare all Your wonderful works.
I will rejoice and boast about You;
I will sing about Your name, Most High.

PSALM 9:1–2 HCSB

Thanks be to God for His indescribable gift.

2 CORINTHIANS 9:15 HCSB

71

Today

This is the day the LORD has made;
let us rejoice and be glad in it.
PSALM 118:24 HCSB

All the days on the calendar have one thing in common: They're all gifts from God. So this day, like every day, is a cause for celebration as we consider God's blessings and His love.

How will you invest this day? Will you treat your time as a commodity too precious to be squandered? Will you carve out time during the day to serve God by serving His children? Will you celebrate God's gifts and obey His commandments? And will you share words of encouragement with the people who cross your path? The answers to these questions will determine, to a surprising extent, the quality of your day and the quality of your life.

So, wherever you find yourself today, take time to celebrate and give thanks for another priceless gift from the Father. The present moment is precious. Treat it that way.

Each day is precious when we consider
what we can do to serve God and His kingdom.
ELIZABETH GEORGE

God's Promises about Today

*But encourage each other every day while
it is "today." Help each other so none of you will
become hardened because sin has tricked you.*
HEBREWS 3:13 NCV

*So don't worry about tomorrow,
because tomorrow will have its own worries.
Each day has enough trouble of its own.*
MATTHEW 6:34 NCV

*There is a time for everything,
and a season for every activity under the heavens.*
ECCLESIASTES 3:1 NIV

*The world and its desires pass away,
but the man who does the will of God lives forever.*
1 JOHN 2:17 NIV

*So teach us to number our days,
that we may present to You a heart of wisdom.*
PSALM 90:12 NASB

72

Trusting God

Trust in the LORD with all your heart, and lean not on your own understanding; in all your ways acknowledge Him, and He shall direct your paths.

PROVERBS 3:5-6 NKJV

Everywhere we turn, or so it seems, people are asking us to trust them. Advertisers and politicians, businesses and governments all proclaim their trustworthiness. And of course many of them are trustworthy. But many of them are not. Oftentimes we are over-promised and underserved. Why? Because mankind is fallen and flawed.

Where will you place your trust today: in fallible humans or in the infallible Creator of the universe? The answer should be obvious.

Today and every day, trust God's promises. Remember that He is always near and that He watches over you. When you are anxious or weak, call upon Him. God can solve your problems better than you can, so turn them over to Him. Remember that the Lord rules both the mountaintops and the valleys—with infinite wisdom and love—now and forever.

Never be afraid to trust an unknown future to a known God.

CORRIE TEN BOOM

God's Promises about Trusting Him

In quietness and trust is your strength.
ISAIAH 30:15 NASB

The LORD is my rock, my fortress, and my deliverer,
my God, my mountain where I seek refuge.
My shield, the horn of my salvation,
my stronghold, my refuge, and my Savior.
2 SAMUEL 22:2–3 HCSB

The fear of man is a snare,
but the one who trusts in the LORD is protected.
PROVERBS 29:25 HCSB

Those who trust in the LORD are like Mount Zion.
It cannot be shaken; it remains forever.
PSALM 125:1 HCSB

Jesus said, "Don't let your hearts be troubled.
Trust in God, and trust in me."
JOHN 14:1 NCV

73

Wisdom and Understanding

*The fear of the LORD is the beginning of knowledge,
but fools despise wisdom and instruction.*
PROVERBS 1:7 NKJV

God's Word makes this promise: If we genuinely desire wisdom, and if we're willing to search for it, we will find it. And where should the search begin? The answer, of course, is in God's holy Word.

The search for wisdom should be a lifelong journey, not a destination. We should continue to read, to watch, and to learn new things as long as we live. But it's not enough to learn new things or to memorize the great Biblical truths; we must also live by them.

So, what will you learn today? Will you take time to feed your mind and fill your heart? And will you study the guidebook that God has given you? Hopefully so, because His plans and His promises are waiting for you there, inside the covers of a book like no other: His Book. It contains the essential wisdom you'll need to navigate the seas of life and land safely on that distant shore.

*If we neglect the Bible, we cannot expect
to benefit from the wisdom and direction
that result from knowing God's Word.*
VONETTE BRIGHT

God's Promises about Wisdom and Understanding

*Get wisdom—how much better it is than gold!
And get understanding—it is preferable to silver.*
PROVERBS 16:16 HCSB

*But the wisdom that is from above is first pure,
then peaceable, gentle, willing to yield, full of mercy and
good fruits, without partiality and without hypocrisy.*
JAMES 3:17 NKJV

*But if any of you lacks wisdom, let him ask of God,
who gives to all generously and without reproach,
and it will be given to him.*
JAMES 1:5 NASB

*Who among you is wise and understanding?
Let him show by his good behavior
his deeds in the gentleness of wisdom.*
JAMES 3:13 NASB

74

Work and Dedication

Whatever you do, do it enthusiastically,
as something done for the Lord and not for men.
Colossians 3:23 HCSB

Time and again, the Bible extols the value of hard work. In Proverbs, we are instructed to take a lesson from a surprising source: ants. Ants are among nature's most industrious creatures. They do their work without supervision, hesitation, or complaint. We should do likewise, but oftentimes we don't. We're tempted to look for shortcuts (there aren't any), or we rely on luck (it happens, but we shouldn't depend on it). Meanwhile, the clock continues to tick, life continues to pass, and important work goes undone.

The book of Proverbs proclaims, "One who is slack in his work is brother to one who destroys" (18:9 NIV). And in his second letter to the Thessalonians, Paul writes, "If any would not work, neither should he eat" (3:10 KJV). In short, God has created a world in which labor is rewarded but laziness is not.

As you think about your own work, please remember that God has big plans for you, and He's given you everything you need to fulfill His purpose. But He won't force His plans upon you, and He won't do all the work. He expects you to do your part. When you do, you'll earn the rewards He most certainly has in store.

All work, if offered to Him, is transformed. It is not secular but sacred, sanctified in the glad offering.

ELISABETH ELLIOT

God's Promises about Work and Dedication

But this I say: He who sows sparingly will also reap sparingly, and he who sows bountifully will also reap bountifully.

2 CORINTHIANS 9:6 NKJV

Be strong and courageous, and do the work. Don't be afraid or discouraged, for the LORD God, my God, is with you. He won't leave you or forsake you.

1 CHRONICLES 28:20 HCSB

The plans of hard-working people earn a profit, but those who act too quickly become poor.

PROVERBS 21:5 NCV

Do you see a man skilled in his work? He will stand in the presence of kings.

PROVERBS 22:29 HCSB

75

Worship

*I was glad when they said unto me,
Let us go into the house of the LORD.*
PSALM 122:1 KJV

Wise women understand the importance of worship. To worship God is a privilege, but it's a privilege that far too many of us forego. Instead of praising our Creator seven days a week, we worship on Sunday mornings (if at all) and spend the rest of the week focusing on other things.

Whenever we become distracted by worldly pursuits that put God in second place, we inevitably pay the price of our misplaced priorities. A better strategy, of course, is to worship Him every day of the week, beginning with a regular early-morning devotional.

Every new day provides another opportunity to worship God with grateful hearts and helping hands. And each day offers another chance to support the church He created. When we do so, we bless others— and we are blessed by the One who sent His only begotten Son so that we might have eternal life.

*Even the most routine part of your day
can be a spiritual act of worship.*
SARAH YOUNG

God's Promises about Worship

Happy are those who hear the joyful call to worship,
for they will walk in the light of your presence, Lord.
PSALM 89:15 NLT

All the earth will worship You and sing praise to You.
They will sing praise to Your name.
PSALM 66:4 HCSB

God is Spirit, and those who worship Him
must worship in spirit and truth.
JOHN 4:24 HCSB

For where two or three are gathered together
in My name, I am there among them.
MATTHEW 18:20 HCSB

Worship the Lord with gladness.
Come before him, singing with joy.
Acknowledge that the Lord is God!
He made us, and we are his.
We are his people, the sheep of his pasture.
PSALM 100:2–3 NLT

LIVE YOUR FAITH

Dear Friend,

This book was prayerfully crafted with you, the reader, in mind—every word, every sentence, every page—was thoughtfully written, designed, and packaged to encourage you...right where you are this very moment. At DaySpring, our vision is to see every person experience the life-changing message of God's love. So, as we worked through rough drafts, design changes, edits and details, we prayed for you to deeply experience His unfailing love, indescribable peace, and pure joy. It is our sincere hope that through these Truth-filled pages your heart will be blessed, knowing that God cares about you—your desires and disappointments, your challenges and dreams.

He knows. He cares. He loves you unconditionally.

BLESSINGS!
THE DAYSPRING BOOK TEAM

———

Additional copies of this book and
other DaySpring titles can be purchased
at fine bookstores everywhere.
Order online at <u>dayspring.com</u>
or
by phone at 1-877-751-4347